Level 1

¡Avancemos!

Unit 8 Resource Book

D1529556

HOLT McDOUGAL
a division of Houghton Mifflin Harcourt

Fine Art Acknowledgments

Page 86 *Paisaje* (undated), Manuel de la Cruz González. Tempera on wood, 33 cm x 29 cm.
Courtesy of Galería 11-12, San José, Costa Rica.

Page 87 *Surcando aires* (2002), Adrián Gómez. Acrílico sobre tela, 55 cm x 75 cm. Courtesy of
the artist.

Page 88 *Midiendo café* (2004), Antonio Mejía. Oil on canvas, 56 cm x 75 cm. Courtesy of Galería
Valanti, San José, Costa Rica.

Page 89 *Familia en el volcán Arenal* (1989), Jeannette Carballo. Oil on canvas. 100 cm x 72 cm.
Courtesy of the artist.

ISBN-13: 978-0-618-76620-8
ISBN-10: 0-618-76620-0   11 12 13 14 1689 18 17 16 15
4500531933
Internet: www.holtmcdougal.com

HOLT McDOUGAL

¡Avancemos!

Table of Contents

To the Teacher

Welcome to *¡Avancemos!* This exciting new Spanish program from McDougal Littell has been designed to provide you—the teacher of today's foreign language classroom—with comprehensive pedagogical support.

PRACTICE WITH A PURPOSE

Activities throughout the program begin by establishing clear goals. Look for the **¡Avanza!** arrow that uses student-friendly language to lead the way towards achievable goals. Built-in self-checks in the student text (**Para y piensa:** Did you get it?) offer the chance to assess student progress throughout the lesson. Both the student text and the workbooks offer abundant leveled practice to match varied student needs.

CULTURE AS A CORNERSTONE

¡Avancemos! celebrates the cultural diversity of the Spanish-speaking world by motivating students to think about similarities and contrasts among different Spanish-speaking cultures. Essential questions encourage thoughtful discussion and comparison between different cultures.

LANGUAGE LEARNING THAT LASTS

The program presents topics in manageable chunks that students will be able to retain and recall. "Recycle" topics are presented frequently so students don't forget material from previous lessons. Previously learned content is built upon and reinforced across the different levels of the program.

TIME-SAVING TEACHER TOOLS

Simplify your planning with McDougal Littell's exclusive teacher resources: the all-inclusive EasyPlanner DVD-ROM, ready-made Power Presentations, and the McDougal Littell Assessment System.

Unit Resource Book

Each Unit Resource Book supports a unit of *¡Avancemos!* The Unit Resource Books provide a wide variety of materials to support, practice, and expand on the material in the *¡Avancemos!* student text.

Components **Following is a list of components included in each Unit Resource Book:**

BACK TO SCHOOL RESOURCES (UNIT 1 ONLY)

Review and start-up activities to support the **Lección preliminar** of the textbook.

DID YOU GET IT? RETEACHING & PRACTICE COPYMASTERS

If students' performance on the **Para y piensa** self-check for a section does not meet your expectations, consider assigning the corresponding Did You Get It? Reteaching and Practice Copymasters. These copymasters provide extensive reteaching and additional practice for every vocabulary and grammar presentation section in *¡Avancemos!* Each vocabulary and grammar section has a corresponding three-page copymaster. The first page of the copymaster reteaches the subject material in a fresh manner. Immediately following this presentation page are two pages of practice exercises that help the student master the topic. The practice pages have engaging contexts and structures to retain students' attention.

PRACTICE GAMES

These games provide fun practice of the vocabulary and grammar just taught. They are targeted in scope so that each game practices a specific area of the **lesson**: *Práctica de vocabulario, Vocabulario en contexto, Práctica de gramática, Gramática en contexto, Todo junto, Repaso de la lección*, and the lesson's cultural information.

Video and audio resources

VIDEO ACTIVITIES

These two-page copymasters accompany the Vocabulary Video and each scene of the **Telehistoria** in Levels 1 and 2 and the **Gran desafío** in Level 3. The pre-viewing activity asks students to activate prior knowledge about a theme or subject related to the scene they will watch. The viewing activity is a simple activity for students to complete as they watch the video. The post-viewing activity gives students the opportunity to demonstrate comprehension of the video episode.

VIDEO SCRIPTS

This section provides the scripts of each video feature in the unit.

AUDIO SCRIPTS

This section contains scripts for all presentations and activities that have accompanying audio in the student text as well as in the two workbooks (*Cuaderno: práctica por niveles* and *Cuaderno para hispanohablantes*) and the assessment program.

Culture resources

MAP/CULTURE ACTIVITIES

This section contains a copymaster with geography and culture activities based on the Unit Opener in the textbook.

FINE ART ACTIVITIES

The fine art activities in every lesson ask students to analyze pieces of art that have been selected as representative of the unit location country. These copymasters can be used in conjunction with the full-color fine art transparencies in the Unit Transparency Book.

Home-school connection

FAMILY LETTERS & FAMILY INVOLVEMENT ACTIVITIES

This section is designed to help increase family support of the students' study of Spanish. The family letter keeps families abreast of the class's progress, while the family involvement activities let students share their Spanish language skills with their families in the context of a game or fun activity.

ABSENT STUDENT COPYMASTERS

The Absent Student Copymasters enable students who miss part of a **lesson** to go over the material on their own. The checkbox format allows teachers to choose and indicate exactly what material the student should complete. The Absent Student Copymasters also offer strategies and techniques to help students understand new or challenging information.

Core Ancillaries in the ¡Avancemos! Program

Leveled workbooks

CUADERNO: PRÁCTICA POR NIVELES

This core ancillary is a leveled practice workbook to supplement the student text. It is designed for use in the classroom or as homework. Students who can complete the activities correctly should be able to pass the quizzes and tests. Practice is organized into three levels of difficulty, labeled A, B, and C. Level B activities are designed to practice vocabulary, grammar, and other core concepts at a level appropriate to most of your students. Students who require more structure can complete Level A activities, while students needing more of a challenge should be encouraged to complete the activities in Level C. Each level provides a different degree of linguistic support, yet requires students to know and handle the same vocabulary and grammar content.

The following sections are included in *Cuaderno: práctica por niveles* for each **lesson**:

Vocabulario A, B, C	Escuchar A, B, C
Gramática 1 A, B, C	Leer A, B, C
Gramática 2 A, B, C	Escribir A, B, C
Integración: Hablar	Cultura A, B, C
Integración: Escribir	

CUADERNO PARA HISPANOHABLANTES

This core ancillary provides leveled practice for heritage learners of Spanish. Level A is for heritage learners who hear Spanish at home but who may speak little Spanish themselves. Level B is for those who speak some Spanish but don't read or write it yet and who may lack formal education in Spanish. Level C is for heritage learners who have had some formal schooling in Spanish. These learners can read and speak Spanish, but may need further development of their writing skills. The *Cuaderno para hispanohablantes* will ensure that heritage learners practice the same basic grammar, reading, and writing skills taught in the student text. At the same time, it offers additional instruction and challenging practice designed specifically for students with prior knowledge of Spanish.

The following sections are included in *Cuaderno para hispanohablantes* for each **lesson**:

Vocabulario A, B, C	Integración: Hablar
Vocabulario adicional	Integración: Escribir
Gramática 1 A, B, C	Lectura A, B, C
Gramática 2 A, B, C	Escritura A, B, C
Gramática adicional	Cultura A, B, C

Other Ancillaries

ASSESSMENT PROGRAM

For each level of *¡Avancemos!*, there are four complete assessment options. Every option assesses students' ability to use the lesson and unit vocabulary and grammar, as well as assessing reading, writing, listening, speaking, and cultural knowledge. The on-level tests are designed to assess the language skills of most of your students. Modified tests provide more support, explanation and scaffolding to enable students with learning difficulties to produce language at the same level as their peers. Pre-AP* tests build the test-taking skills essential to success on Advanced Placement tests. The assessments for heritage learners are all in Spanish, and take into account the strengths that native speakers bring to language learning.

In addition to leveled lesson and unit tests, there is a complete array of vocabulary, culture, and grammar quizzes. All tests include scoring rubrics and point teachers to specific resources for remediation.

UNIT TRANSPARENCY BOOKS—1 PER UNIT

Each transparency book includes:

- Map Atlas Transparencies (Unit 1 only)
- Unit Opener Map Transparencies
- Fine Art Transparencies
- Vocabulary Transparencies
- Grammar Presentation Transparencies
- Situational Transparencies with Label Overlay (plus student copymasters)
- Warm Up Transparencies
- Student Book and Workbook Answer Transparencies

LECTURAS PARA TODOS

A workbook-style reader, *Lecturas para todos*, offers all the readings from the student text as well as additional literary readings in an interactive format. In addition to the readings, they contain reading strategies, comprehension questions, and tools for developing vocabulary.

There are four sections in each *Lecturas para todos*:

- *¡Avancemos!* readings with annotated skill-building support
- *Literatura adicional*—additional literary readings
- Academic and Informational Reading Development
- Test Preparation Strategies

* AP and the Advanced Placement Program are registered trademarks of the College Entrance Examination Board, which was not involved in the production of and does not endorse this product.

LECTURAS PARA HISPANOHABLANTES

Lecturas para hispanohablantes offers additional cultural readings for heritage learners and a rich selection of literary readings. All readings are supported by reading strategies, comprehension questions, tools for developing vocabulary, plus tools for literary analysis.

There are four sections in each *Lecturas para hispanohablantes*:

- *En voces* cultural readings with annotated skill-building support

- *Literatura adicional*—high-interest readings by prominent authors from around the Spanish-speaking world. Selections were chosen carefully to reflect the diversity of experiences Spanish-speakers bring to the classroom.

- Bilingual Academic and Informational Reading Development

- Bilingual Test Preparation Strategies, for success on standardized tests in English

COMIC BOOKS

These fun, motivating comic books are written in a contemporary, youthful style with full-color illustrations. Each comic uses the target language students are learning. There is one 32-page comic book for each level of the program.

TPRS: TEACHING PROFICIENCY THROUGH READING AND STORYTELLING

This book includes an up-to-date guide to TPRS and TPRS stories written by Piedad Gutiérrez that use *¡Avancemos!* lesson-specific vocabulary.

MIDDLE SCHOOL RESOURCE BOOK

- Practice activities to support the 1b Bridge lesson
- Diagnostic and Bridge Unit Tests
- Transparencies
  - Vocabulary Transparencies
  - Grammar Transparencies
  - Answer Transparencies for the Student Text
  - Bridge Warm Up Transparencies
- Audio CDs

LESSON PLANS

- Lesson Plans with suggestions for modifying instruction
- Core and Expansion options clearly noted
- IEP suggested modifications
- Substitute teacher lesson plans

BEST PRACTICES TOOLKIT

Strategies for Effective Teaching

- Research-based Learning Strategies
- Language Learning that Lasts: Teaching for Long-term Retention
- Culture as a Cornerstone/Cultural Comparisons
- English Grammar Connection
- Building Vocabulary
- Developing Reading Skills
- Differentiation
- Best Practices in Teaching Heritage Learners
- Assessment (including Portfolio Assessment, Reteaching and Remediation)
- Best Practices Swap Shop: Favorite Activities for Teaching Reading, Writing, Listening, Speaking
- Reading, Writing, Listening, and Speaking Strategies in the World Languages classroom
- ACTFL Professional Development Articles
- Thematic Teaching
- Best Practices in Middle School

Using Technology in the World Languages Classroom
Tools for Motivation

- Games in the World Languages Classroom
- Teaching Proficiency through Reading and Storytelling
- Using Comic Books for Motivation

Pre-AP and International Baccalaureate

- International Baccalaureate
- Pre-AP

Graphic Organizer Transparencies

- Teaching for Long-term Retention
- Teaching Culture
- Building Vocabulary
- Developing Reading Skills

Absent Student Copymasters—Tips for Students

LISTENING TO CDS AT HOME

- Open your text, workbook, or class notes to the corresponding pages that relate to the audio you will listen to. Read the assignment directions if there are any. Do these steps before listening to the audio selections.

- Listen to the CD in a quiet place. Play the CD loudly enough so that you can hear everything clearly. Keep focused. Play a section several times until you understand it. Listen carefully. Repeat aloud with the CD. Try to sound like the people on the CD. Stop the CD when you need to do so.

- If you are lost, stop the CD. Replay it and look at your notes. Take a break if you are not focusing. Return and continue after a break. Work in short periods of time: 5 or 10 minutes at a time so that you remain focused and energized.

QUESTION/ANSWER SELECTIONS

- If there is a question/answer selection, read the question aloud several times. Write down the question. Highlight the key words, verb endings, and any new words. Look up new words and write their meaning. Then say everything aloud.

- One useful strategy for figuring out questions is to put parentheses around groups of words that go together. For example: **(¿Cuántos niños)(van)(al estadio)(a las tres?)** Read each group of words one at a time. Check for meaning. Write out answers. Highlight key words and verb endings. Say the question aloud. Read the answer aloud. Ask yourself if you wrote what you meant.

- Be sure to say everything aloud several times before moving on to the next question. Check for spelling, verb endings, and accent marks.

FLASHCARDS FOR VOCABULARY

- If you have Internet access, go to ClassZone at classzone.com. All the vocabulary taught in *¡Avancemos!* is available on electronic flashcards. Look for the flashcards in the *¡Avancemos!* section of ClassZone.

- If you don't have Internet access, write the Spanish word or phrase on one side of a 3″ × 5″ card, and the English translation on the other side. Illustrate your flashcards when possible. Be sure to highlight any verb endings, accent marks, or other special spellings that will need a bit of extra attention.

GRAMMAR ACTIVITIES

- Underline or highlight all verb endings and adjective agreements. For example:
  Nosotros comemos pollo rico.

- Underline or highlight infinitive endings: **trabajar**.

- Underline or highlight accented letters. Say aloud and be louder on the accented letters. Listen carefully for the loudness. This will remind you where to write your accent mark. For example: **lápiz, lápices, árbol, árboles**

- When writing a sentence, be sure to ask yourself, "What do I mean? What am I trying to say?" Then check your sentence to be sure that you wrote what you wanted to say.

- Mark patterns with a highlighter. For example, for stem-changing verbs, you can draw a "boot" around the letters that change:

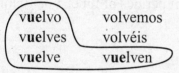

READING AND CULTURE SECTIONS

- Read the strategy box. Copy the graphic organizer so you can fill it out as you read.

- Look at the title and subtitles before you begin to read. Then look at and study any photos and read the captions. Translate the captions only if you can't understand them at all. Before you begin to read, guess what the selection will be about. What do you think that you will learn? What do you already know about this topic?

- Read any comprehension questions before beginning to read the paragraphs. This will help you focus on the upcoming reading selection. Copy the questions and highlight key words.

- Reread one or two of the questions and then go to the text. Begin to read the selection carefully. Read it again. On a sticky note, write down the appropriate question number next to where the answer lies in the text. This will help you keep track of what the questions have asked you and will help you focus when you go back to reread it later, perhaps in preparation for a quiz or test.

- Highlight any new words. Make a list or flashcards of new words. Look up their meanings. Study them. Quiz yourself or have a partner quiz you. Then go back to the comprehension questions and check your answers from memory. Look back at the text if you need to verify your answers.

PAIRED PRACTICE EXERCISES

- If there is an exercise for partners, practice both parts at home.

- If no partner is available, write out both scripts and practice both roles aloud. Highlight and underline key words, verb endings, and accent marks.

WRITING PROJECTS

- Brainstorm ideas before writing.

- Make lists of your ideas.

- Put numbers next to the ideas to determine the order in which you want to write about them.

- Group your ideas into paragraphs.

- Skip lines in your rough draft.

- Have a partner read your work and give you feedback on the meaning and language structure.

- Set it aside and reread it at least once before doing a final draft. Double-check verb endings, adjective agreements, and accents.

- Read it once again to check that you said what you meant to say.

- Be sure to have a title and any necessary illustrations or bibliography.

Did You Get It? *Presentación de vocabulario*

> ▶ **¡AVANZA!**　**Goal:**　Learn words related to daily routines and trips.

Daily Routines

- We all have our own daily routine from the time we wake up until we go to bed. Here are some Spanish words and expressions that name these activities and the items we need to carry them out.

Daily routines	**despertarse** *(to wake up)*
	levantarse *(to get up)*
	vestirse *(to get dressed)*
	ponerse... *(to put on clothes)*
	lavarse la cara *(to wash one's face)*
	cepillarse los dientes *(to brush one's teeth)*
	afeitarse *(to shave oneself)*
	ducharse *(to take a shower)*
	secarse el pelo *(to dry one's hair)*
	peinarse *(to comb one's hair)*
	maquillarse *(to put on makeup)*
	acostarse *(to go to bed)*
	dormirse *(to fall asleep)*
	el cepillo *(brush)*
Personal care	**el cepillo de dientes** *(toothbrush)*
	el champú *(shampoo)*
	el jabón *(soap)*
	el peine *(comb)*
	el secador de pelo *(hair dryer)*
	la pasta de dientes *(toothpaste)*
	la toalla *(towel)*

Taking a Trip

- Usually **(Normalmente)**, we all like vacations **(las vacaciones)**! Generally **(Generalmente)**, we also all like to take a trip **(hacer un viaje)**. Read and study the following words that will help you talk about being on vacation **(de vacaciones)**.

Where to go	**la ciudad** *(city)*	*How to go*	**en tren** *(by train)*
	el campo *(country)*		**en barco** *(by boat)*

UNIDAD 8 Lección 1　Reteaching and Practice

Did You Get It? *Práctica de vocabulario*

¡AVANZA!   **Goal:** Learn words related to daily routines and trips.

1 Choose the object that you use to do the following things.

el secador de pelo	el champú	el jabón
la toalla	el cepillo	el cepillo de dientes

1. wash your hair _____

2. wash your face _____

3. brush your hair _____

4. dry your hair _____

5. brush your teeth _____

6. dry yourself _____

2 Which activity do you do...

1. before going to bed?   levantarse   dormirse   cepillarse los dientes

2. in the morning?   despertarse   acostarse   dormirse

3. after a shower?   lavarse la cara   secarse   levantarse

4. after being in the wind? afeitarse   peinarse   acostarse

5. before going to a party? vestirse   acostarse   dormirse

6. after going to bed?   maquillarse   levantarse   dormirse

3 How do these people travel and where do they go? Follow the model.

Modelo: Enrique / el campo / tren
          Enrique hace un viaje al campo en tren.

1. Mario y Luisa / la ciudad / coche

   _____

2. los estudiantes / España / barco

   _____

3. Mi familia y yo / el campo / tren

   _____

4 Which items do you need for each routine?

1. lavarse la cara o ducharse _____

2. cepillarse los dientes _____

3. lavarse el pelo _____

4. secarse el pelo _____

5. peinarse _____

6. secarse después de ducharse _____

5 Complete each sentence with a word or phrase from the box.

| normalmente maquillarse acostarse la cara jabón la toalla los dientes champú |

1. Todas las noches me gusta lavarme _____ .

2. Me gusta cepillarme _____ después de comer.

3. Compro un _____ nuevo para lavarme el pelo.

4. A Luisa le gusta _____ antes de salir.

5. Rogelio quiere _____ porque está cansado.

6. Prefiero secarme el pelo con _____, no con el secador.

7. _____ me gusta afeitarme en la mañana.

8. Me lavo la cara con un _____ especial.

6 Decide whether each statement is logical (**L**) or illogical (**I**).

1. A Susana le gusta levantarse inmediatamente después de despertarse.   L   I

2. Lola prefiere lavarse la cara con el secador de pelo.   L   I

3. Jorge quiere afeitarse después de levantarse.   L   I

4. Los chicos quieren cepillarse los dientes con la toalla.   L   I

5. A ella le gusta lavarse la cara, cepillarse los dientes y acostarse.   L   I

6. Las chicas prefieren maquillarse antes de lavarse la cara.   L   I

7 Write three things you generally like to do every day and the order in which you like to do them. Follow the model.

Modelo: *Generalmente me gusta levantarme a las siete y media. Me gusta lavarme la cara antes de vestirme. Me gusta ponerme la ropa antes de peinarme.*

_____

_____

_____

Did You Get It? *Presentación de gramática*

> **¡AVANZA!** **Goal:** Learn how to form and use reflexive verbs to describe daily routines.

Reflexive Verbs

- *Reflexive verbs* show that the subject of a sentence both does and receives the action of the verb. The reflexive pronouns in English end in *-self* or *-selves*. Read the following sentences, paying special attention to the boldfaced words.

  Yo **me** levanté a las siete. (I got *myself* up at seven o'clock.)

  Ella **se** levantó a las nueve. (She got *herself* up at nine o'clock.)

  Ustedes **se** levantaron a las once. (You got *yourselves* up at eleven o'clock.)

EXPLANATION: In Spanish, all reflexive verbs are expressed with a *reflexive pronoun*. Study the conjugation of **levantarse** below.

yo   **me** levanto *(I get **myself** up)*

tú   **te** levantas *(you get **yourself** up)*

él/ella/usted **se** levanta *(he/she/you get **himself/herself/yourself** up)*

nosotros(as) **nos** levantamos *(we get **ourselves** up)*

vosotros(as) **os** levantáis *(you get **yourselves** up)*

ellos(as)/ustedes **se** levantan *(they/you get **themselves/yourselves** up)*

- Study these sentences, paying attention to the boldfaced words.

  Linda **se maquilla.** ⟶ *Linda puts on makeup (**makes herself up**).*

  Linda **maquilla a su amiga.** ⟶ *Linda **puts makeup on her friend (makes her friend up).***

EXPLANATION: Some verbs are not always reflexive. Also, some verbs have different meanings when used reflexively. For example,

dormir *(to sleep)* ⟶ **dormirse** *(to fall asleep)*
poner *(to put)* ⟶ **ponerse** *(to put on (clothes))*

- Read these sentences in Spanish, paying attention to the boldfaced words.

  ¿A qué hora **vas** a despertar**te**?   ⎱ *What time are you going to wake*
  ¿A qué hora **te vas** a despertar?   ⎰ *(yourself) up?*

EXPLANATION: Reflexive pronouns can be *attached* to the *infinitive form* of a reflexive verb, or come *before* the *conjugated verb*.

Did You Get It? *Práctica de gramática*

┃**¡AVANZA!**┃ **Goal:** Learn how to form and use reflexive verbs to describe daily routines.

❶ Fill in the correct reflexive pronoun for the subject.

Modelo: Yo _me_ lavo.

1. Ella _____ levanta.

2. Anita y yo _____ maquillamos.

3. Tú _____ afeitas.

4. Usted _____ pone la ropa.

5. Ustedes _____ despiertan.

6. Ellas _____ maquillan.

7. Nosotros _____ lavamos el pelo.

8. Él _____ ducha.

9. Ellos _____ acuestan.

10. Tú y yo _____ dormimos.

❷ Form sentences using the words given. Follow the model.

Modelo: Yo / acostarse tarde

Yo me acuesto tarde.

1. usted / ponerse la chaqueta nueva

   _____

2. Vanesa y tú / cepillarse muy rápido los dientes

   _____

3. Silvia / ponerse un vestido elegante

   _____

4. Ana y su hermana / maquillarse demasiado

   _____

5. Yo / lavarse la cara todas las mañanas

   _____

6. mi hermana y yo / acostarse temprano

   _____

❸ Form sentences with the words given. Follow the model.

Modelo: ellos / querer lavarse el pelo

Ellos quieren lavarse el pelo.

1. María / querer levantarse a las ocho

_____

2. tú / querer acostarse temprano

_____

3. Lisa y yo / querer maquillarse antes de salir

_____

4. Paco / querer afeitarse antes de ir a la fiesta

_____

5. Marielsa y tú / querer despertarse tarde

_____

❹ Form sentences using the words given. Follow the model.

Modelo: Yo quiero levantarme temprano.

Yo me quiero levantar temprano.

1. Ustedes quieren cepillarse los dientes después de comer.

_____

2. Usted quiere bañarse en la mañana.

_____

3. Tú quieres despertarte a las ocho mañana.

_____

4. Nosotras queremos maquillarnos antes de salir

_____

❺ Translate the following pairs of sentences into Spanish.

1. José Antonio washes his hands. _____

Arturo washes his car. _____

2. Andrea puts on her jacket. _____

Luisa puts the plate on the table. _____

3. Tomeu sleeps in the car. _____

Alison falls asleep at ten. _____

Did You Get It? *Presentación de gramática*

> **¡AVANZA!**   **Goal:**   Learn how to form the present progressive tense.

Present Progressive

- As in English, the *present progressive tense* in Spanish is used to talk about what is happening right now. Study the chart, paying attention to the boldfaced words.

escuchar	Estoy **escuchando** música.	*(**I am listening** to music.)*
comer	¿Qué **estás comiendo**?	*(What **are you eating**?)*
compartir	Ellos **están compartiendo** una pizza.	*(They **are sharing** a pizza.)*

EXPLANATION: You use the present tense of **estar** + present participle to form the present progressive tense. You form the present participle (the Spanish **gerundio**) by dropping the ending from the infinitive and adding **-ando** to **-ar** verbs or **-iendo** to **-er** and **-ir** verbs.

- Read these sentences.

le -er	Ana **está leyendo** un libro.	*(Ana **is reading** a book.)*
tra-er	Ellos **están trayendo** los regalos.	*(They **are bringing** the gifts.)*

EXPLANATION: When the stem of an **-er** or **-ir** verb ends with a vowel, **-iendo** becomes **-yendo**.

- Now study these present participles.

pedir	⟶	pidiendo
servir	⟶	sirviendo
vestir	⟶	vistiendo
decir	⟶	diciendo
venir	⟶	viniendo
dormir	⟶	durmiendo

EXPLANATION: Some **-ir** verbs change vowels in the stem of the present participle form.

- Finally, read these sentences.

Me estoy peinando.
Estoy peinándome.   } *(I am combing my hair.)*

EXPLANATION: *Pronouns* can be placed *before* the conjugated form of **estar** or *attached* to the end of the *present participle* (or **gerundio**). When a pronoun is attached to the present participle, an *accent* is needed to keep the original stress.

Did You Get It? *Práctica de gramática*

> **¡AVANZA!** **Goal:** Learn how to form the present progressive tense.

❶ Form the present participle (**gerundio**) of each verb.

1. caminar _____   7. correr _____

2. despertar _____   8. dormir _____

3. afeitar _____   9. traer _____

4. maquillar _____   10. hacer _____

5. bañar _____   11. decir _____

6. lavar _____   12. beber _____

❷ Complete each sentence with the correct form of the present participle of the verb in parentheses.

1. Yo estoy _____ un viaje. (**hacer**)

2. Elisa está _____ el sol. (**tomar**)

3. Migdalia y su amiga están _____ en un restaurante. (**comer**)

4. Los señores Tobar están _____ al tren. (**subir**)

5. Yo estoy _____ con mi hermano. (**jugar**)

6. Ellos están _____ un refresco. (**beber**)

7. Felipe está _____ las maletas. (**traer**)

8. Ustedes están _____ la televisión. (**ver**)

❸ What is everyone doing? Answer the questions using the model as a guide.

Modelo: ¿Estás afeitándote? (**cepillarse los dientes**)
   No, me estoy cepillando los dientes.

1. ¿Ustedes están lavándose? (**cepillarse los dientes**)

   _____

2. ¿Estás duchándote? (**maquillarse**)

   _____

3. ¿Los niños están levantándose? (**despertarse**)

   _____

4. ¿Estoy maquillándome bien? (**ponerse mucho maquillaje**)

   _____

5. ¿Aldo todavía está lavándose el pelo? (**peinarse**)

   _____

4 Look at the pictures to say what each person is doing on vacation.

Modelo:  la mujer

La mujer se está poniendo la chaqueta.

1.   **2.**   **3.**   **4.**   **5.**   **6.**

1. el chico _____

2. mi padre _____

3. mi amiga _____

4. José y Lupe _____

5. la señora López _____

6. las chicas _____

5 Complete the sentences to state what you normally are doing at different times of the day. Follow the model.

Modelo: A las seis de la mañana   *estoy durmiendo.*

1. A las siete de la mañana _____

2. A las nueve de la mañana _____

3. A las doce y media de la tarde _____

4. A las cuatro de la tarde _____

5. A las siete de la tarde _____

6. A las nueve de la noche _____

7. A las once de la noche _____

8. A las tres de la mañana _____

♻ ¿Recuerdas?

Level 1 pp. 412, 421, 424
Level 1B pp. 231, 241, 245

Preterite Of Hacer, Chores, Telling Time

- Review the preterite tense of **hacer** (*to do, to make*) and four expressions using the verb.

hacer (to do, to make)	
hice	hicimos
hiciste	hicisteis
hizo	hicieron

hacer la cama (*to make the bed*)
hacer la tarea (*to do homework*)
hacer un pastel (*to make a cake*)
hacer un viaje (*to take a trip*)

- Review the names of these rooms in a house.

el baño (*the bathroom*)   **la cocina** (*the kitchen*)
el cuarto (*the bedroom*)   **la sala** (*the living room*)

- Read the time shown on these clocks.

Son las diez.   **Son las once y media.**   **Son las siete menos veinte.**   **Son las once y diez.**   **Son las dos y cuarto.**   **Son las doce.**

Práctica

① Translate the following sentences into Spanish.

1. I took a trip by train at 7:30.

_____

2. Ana made the bed at 10:40.

_____

3. You did your homework at 6:20.

_____

4. We swept the kitchen floor at 4:10.

_____

5. You watched TV in the living room at 9:00.

_____

6. He cleaned the bathroom at 7:15.

_____

¿Recuerdas?

Level 1 p. 414
Level 1B p. 233

Direct object pronouns

- Read the following sentences, paying attention to the boldfaced words. Then, review the chart below that contains all of the direct object pronouns in Spanish.

Voy a usar **el secador**. ⟶
*(I am going to use **the dryer**.)*

Voy a usar**lo**.
or
Lo voy a usar.

(I am going to use it.)

Direct object pronouns	
Singular	**Plural**
me *(me)*	**nos** *(us)*
te *(you familiar)*	**os** *(you familiar)*
lo *(you formal/him/it)*	**los** *(you formal/them masculine)*
la *(you formal/them feminine)*	**las** *(you formal/them feminine)*

Práctica

➊ Write the direct object pronoun that corresponds to each noun. The first one is done for you.

1. la ciudad *la*

2. el campo _____

3. el cepillo _____

4. las toallas _____

5. el jabón _____

6. tú y yo _____

7. los chicos _____

8. el peine _____

9. tú, Julia _____

10. yo _____

➋ What did Ana take on vacation? Follow the model.

Modelo: ¿Llevó la pasta de dientes?   *Sí, la llevó.*

1. ¿Llevó el cepillo de dientes? _____

2. ¿Llevó el secador de pelo? _____

3. ¿Llevó la chaqueta? _____

4. ¿Llevó a su gata? _____

5. ¿Llevó las toallas? _____

6. ¿Llevó el champú? _____

7. ¿Llevó su jabón favorito? _____

8. ¿Llevó a sus amigos? _____

UNIDAD 8 Lección 1

Reteaching and Practice

 ¿Recuerdas?

Parts Of The Body

• Study the names of the following parts of the body in Spanish.

El cuerpo *(the body)*			
la boca *(mouth)*	el corazón *(heart)*	el ojo *(eye)*	la pierna *(leg)*
el brazo *(arm)*	el estómago *(stomach)*	la oreja *(ear)*	la rodilla *(knee)*
la cabeza *(head)*	la mano *(hand)*	el pie *(foot)*	el tobillo *(ankle)*
la cara *(face)*	la nariz *(nose)*	la piel *(skin)*	los dientes *(teeth)*

Práctica

1 Which part of the body is being described?

1. La usamos para oler *(to smell)*. _____

2. La usamos para pensar. _____

3. La usamos para hablar. _____

4. Las usamos para caminar. _____

5. Los usamos para ver. _____

6. La usamos para escribir. _____

2 Tell what each person is washing. Follow the model.

Modelo:  Linda
Linda se está lavando la cara.

 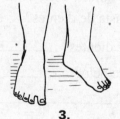 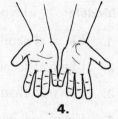

1.   **2.**   **3.**   **4.**

1. José _____

2. tú _____

3. yo _____

4. Aldo y yo _____

Did You Get It? *Presentación de vocabulario*

 ¡AVANZA!   **Goal:**   Learn about vacation activities and buying souvenirs.

Vacation Activities

- Everyone likes a vacation! Read these words and expressions that will help you talk about the different activities you can do while on vacation.

> **comer al aire libre** *(to picnic, to eat outside)*
>
> **hacer surfing** *(to surf)*
>
> **hacer surf de vela** *(to windsurf)*
>
> **acampar** *(to camp)*
>
> **montar a caballo** *(to ride horses)*
>
> **hacer una parrillada** *(to barbecue)*
>
> **dar una caminata** *(to hike)*

Buying Souvenirs

- The local markets where you're visiting are fun places to shop. Read the following e–mail to learn several words and expressions you can use to talk about what you can buy.

A: Jorge
De: Isabel

Hola, Jorge:

This summer I would like to **(quisiera)** visit new places and shop at the local markets **(mercados)**. There you can find many souvenirs **(recuerdos)**, including jewelry **(joyas)** such as necklaces **(collares)**, silver earrings **(aretes de plata)**, and gold rings **(anillos de oro)**. Also, you can find handicrafts **(artesanías)** such as ceramics **(cerámicas)** and articles made of wood **(artículos de madera)**. Many of these items are of good quality **(calidad)** and often inexpensive **(baratos)**. It's important to know how to bargain **(regatear)** to make sure that you don't pay too much **(demasiado)**! And you, what are your plans for the summer?

Tu amiga,

Isabel

Did You Get It? *Práctica de vocabulario*

> **¡AVANZA!**   **Goal:**   Learn about vacation activities and buying souvenirs.

❶ What does each person buy? Follow the model.

Modelo:

Ana

Ana compra un artículo de madera.

1.

2.

3.

4.

1. tú _____

2. mi padre _____

3. yo _____

4. mis amigos _____

❷ Complete the paragraph with appropriate vocabulary words.

de plata	collar	barato	quisiera	calidad	demasiado

Alicia: Buenos días. _____ comprar un regalo para una amiga.

¿Puedo ver los aretes _____ , por favor?

Vendedor: Sí, claro. Son muy bonitos y de muy buena _____ .

Alicia: ¿Cuánto cuestan?

Vendedor: Diez mil quinientos colones.

Alicia: ¡Diez mil quinientos! ¡Es _____ ! Tengo ocho mil.

¿Tiene algo más _____ ?

Vendedor: Sí, el _____ de madera cuesta ocho mil.

Alicia: También es bonito. Lo compro.

❸ Complete each sentence with an appropriate vocabulary word.

1. A Susana le gustan los aretes. Los lleva en las _____ .

2. A mi papá le gusta la _____ . Va a comprar el plato.

3. A mi hermana le gusta este anillo. Lo va a llevar en el _____ .

4. A mi abuela le gustan las _____ . Va a comprar un collar de plata.

5. Estoy de vacaciones. Voy a comprar unos _____ para mis amigos.

6. Quiero ir al _____ . Tengo que comprar un regalo de cumpleaños.

7. El artículo de plata es bonito. Es de buena _____ .

8. El anillo de oro cuesta demasiado. Voy a _____ con el vendedor.

❹ What does each person do on vacation? Follow the model.

Modelo:  _Luisa hace surfing._

Luisa

1. los chicos   **2. mi hermana**   **3. los amigos**   **4. mis padres**   **5. ustedes**

1. _____

2. _____

3. _____

4. _____

5. _____

❺ Name three things that you like to do while on vacation.

_____

_____

_____

Did You Get It? *Presentación de gramática*

> **¡AVANZA!** **Goal:** Use indirect object pronouns to discuss gifts.

Indirect Object Pronouns

- Indirect object pronouns are nouns or pronouns that tell *to whom* or *for whom* the action in a sentence takes place. Read the following sentences, paying special attention to the boldfaced words.

Mi abuela **me** da un regalo.	*(My grandmother gives a gift **to me**.)*
Te doy un regalo.	*(I give a gift **to you**.)*
Le damos un regalo.	*(We give a gift **to him / her / you**.)*

EXPLANATION: Use indirect object pronouns to say *to whom* or *for whom* an action takes place.

Singular		Plural	
me	*me*	**nos**	*us*
te	*you (familiar)*	**os**	*you (familiar)*
le	*you (formal), him, her*	**les**	*you, them*

- Read these sentences, paying attention to the boldfaced words.

Le doy el regalo.	**Le** doy el regalo a **José**.
*(I give the **gift to him / her / you**.)*	*(I give the gift **to José**.)*
Les doy los regalos.	**Les** doy los regalos **a Andrés** y **a Pilar.**
*(I give the gifts to **them / you**.)*	*(I give the gifts to **Andrés and Pilar**.)*

EXPLANATION: The pronouns **le** and **les** refer to one or more people. To clarify what they mean, they are often accompanied by **a** + *noun or pronoun*.

- Study these sentences, paying attention to the boldfaced words.

Les voy a comprar regalos a mis amigos.
Voy a comprar**les** regalos a mis amigos.

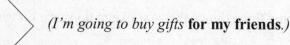

*(I'm going to buy gifts **for my friends**.)*

EXPLANATION: When a conjugated verb is followed by an infinitive, the pronoun can be placed *before* the *conjugated verb* or *attached* to the end of the *infinitive*.

Did You Get It? *Práctica de gramática*

> **¡AVANZA!**   **Goal:**   Use indirect object pronouns to discuss gifts.

❶ Which indirect pronoun would you use for the italicized words?

me	te	le	nos	os	les

1. John always tells *me* secrets. _____
2. I'm going to buy *her* a birthday gift. _____
3. Did your sister give *you* the money? _____
4. They tell *us* where to buy inexpensive jewelry. _____
5. I thank *them* every day. _____

❷ Choose the correct indirect object pronoun to complete each sentence.

1. Ella (me / nos) compra un recuerdo a mí.
2. Tú (le / nos) dices el secreto a nosotros.
3. ¿Por qué (te / le) das el regalo a él?
4. Nosotros (les / te) compramos un anillo de plata a ti.
5. Tus amigos (les / me) dan los collares a ti y a Julia.
6. Miguel (me / le) da aretes de plata a Susana.
7. Ustedes (les / le) dan la información a sus amigos.
8. ¿Cuándo (te / me) vas a dar el regalo a mí?

❸ Change each sentence, using the model as a guide.

Modelo: Voy a comprarte un recuerdo. *Te voy a comprar un recuerdo.*

1. Ustedes van a comprarles un regalo.

   _____

2. ¿Vas a comprarle los aretes para su cumpleaños?

   _____

3. Vas a comprarnos el DVD para la fiesta.

   _____

4. No quiero comprarte el collar en el mercado.

   _____

5. Óscar va a comprarme un anillo de plata para mi cumpleaños.

   _____

UNIDAD 8 Lección 2

Reteaching and Practice

4 Complete the telephone conversation with the correct indirect object pronouns.

Ariana: Hola, Enrique. Acabo de volver de mis vacaciones en la República Dominicana.

Enrique: ¿Qué tal el viaje? ¿Te gustó? Y a nosotros, ¿ _____ trajiste muchos recuerdos?

Ariana: Sí, _____ compré recuerdos a todos. _____ compré un anillo de plata a Susana. _____ compré unos collares de madera a Lupe y a Luisa. _____ compré un artículo de madera a Jorge...

Enrique: Y a mí, ¿qué _____ compraste?

Ariana: A ti _____ compré el mejor regalo de todos.

5 Write sentences explaining who bought what for whom. Follow the model.

Modelo: Anita / comprar un regalo / a mí   *Anita me compró un regalo a mí.*

1. María / comprar aretes / a su madre

   _____

2. tú / comprar un anillo / a mí

   _____

3. Lucía y yo / comprar artículos de cerámica / a nuestros amigos.

   _____

4. ustedes / comprar unos collares / a nosotras

   _____

5. Paco / comprar un DVD / a ti

   _____

6. Marielsa y tú / comprar un disco compacto / a su primo

   _____

7. nosotros / comprar un regalo / a ellos

   _____

6 Translate the following sentences into Spanish.

1. You bought him a ring. _____

2. We bought them DVDs. _____

3. I bought you a silver necklace. _____

4. Did they buy us souvenirs from their trip? _____

5. You (**ustedes**) bought gifts for your friends. _____

Did You Get It? *Presentación de gramática*

> **¡AVANZA!**   **Goal:**   Learn how to use demonstrative adjectives.

Demonstrative Adjectives

- Demonstrative adjectives are words that help you point out specific things. Read the following sentences, paying attention to the boldfaced words.

¿Te gusta **este** anillo que está aquí?   *(Do you like **this** ring here?)*

No. Me gusta **ese** anillo.   *(No. I like **that** ring.)*

Aquel anillo es bonito también.   **(That** *ring* **over there** *is pretty too.)*

EXPLANATION: Demonstrative adjectives indicate the location of a person or thing in relation to the speaker. **Este** and **estos** *(this, these)* refer to what is near the speaker. **Ese** and **esos** *(that, those)* refer to what is near the person addressed. **Aquel** and **aquellos** *(that, those)* refer to what is far from both the speaker and the person addressed. All demonstrative adjectives go *before* the noun they describe and agree with the noun in gender and number. Study the chart below and use it as a quick reference for all forms of demonstrative adjectives.

Masculine				
Singular		**Plural**		**Location**
este collar	**this** *necklace*	**estos** collares	**these** *necklaces*	*near the speaker*
ese collar	**that** *necklace*	**esos** collares	**those** *necklaces*	*near the person addressed*
aquel collar	**that** *necklace (over there)*	**aquellos** collares	**those** *necklaces (over there)*	*far from the speaker and the person addressed*

Feminine				
Singular		**Plural**		**Location**
esta blusa	**this** *blouse*	**estas** blusas	**these** *blouses*	*near the speaker*
esa blusa	**that** *blouse*	**esas** blusas	**those** *blouses*	*near the person addressed*
aquella blusa	**that** *blouse (over there)*	**aquellas** blusas	**those** *blouses (over there)*	*far from the speaker and the person addressed*

Did You Get It? *Práctica de gramática*

¡AVANZA! **Goal:** Learn how to use demonstrative adjectives.

❶ Write the correct demonstrative adjective for the nouns in each group.

1. ¿**este** o **esta**? *(this)*

joya	mercado
arete de oro	artesanía
camiseta	artículo de madera

2. ¿**ese** o **esa**? *(that)*

camisa	anillo de plata
collar de madera	recuerdo
arete	artesanía de metal

3. ¿**aquel** o **aquella**? *(that over there)*

anillo de oro	camisa roja
recuerdo	collar de oro
mercado de artesanías	joya

4. ¿**estos** o **estas**? *(these)*

camisas azules	mercados
faldas cortas	artículos de madera
aretes de plata	artesanías baratas

5. ¿**esos** o **esas**? *(those there)*

collares rojos	recuerdos
mercados	sombreros marrones
chaquetas cortas	artículos

6. ¿**aquellos** o **aquellas**? *(those over there)*

camisetas blancas	artículos de madera
anillos de plata	pantalones cortos
joyas baratas	mercados

❷ Choose the correct demonstrative adjective to complete the paragraph.

Olivia: (Esos / Esas) joyas son bonitas. ¿Puedo ver (aquel / aquella) anillo?

Vendedor: ¡Claro que sí! Es barato. Cuesta veinte mil colones.

Olivia: ¿Veinte mil colones? Es muy caro. ¿Y (estos / estas) aretes de aquí? ¿Cuánto cuestan?

Vendedor: Son más baratos. Cuestan diez mil colones.

Olivia: Los aretes son caros también. ¿Y (ese / esa) collar? ¡Tiene que ser barato!

Vendedor: Sí, es la más barata de todas las joyas.

Olivia: Está bien. Compro (ese / esa) collar.

❸ Change the demonstrative adjectives to the singular or to the plural, making all necessary changes. Follow the model.

Modelo: Este anillo es barato. *Estos anillos son baratos.*
Esas faldas son cortas. *Esa falda es corta.*

1. Aquella chaqueta es bonita. _____
2. Ese mercado vende joyas bonitas. _____
3. Esta artesanía es demasiado cara. _____
4. ¿Compro estos collares de oro? _____
5. Aquellos recuerdos son baratos. _____

❹ Translate the following sentences into English.

1. Esta caminata me cansó mucho. _____
2. Esos recuerdos son de buena calidad. _____
3. ¿Es de oro o de plata esta artesanía? _____
4. Aquellas joyas cuestan demasiado. _____
5. ¿Debo comprar este anillo o aquellos aretes? _____

❺ Translate the following sentences into Spanish.

1. This market sells many souvenirs. _____
2. Those earrings cost too much. _____
3. How much does that ring over there cost? _____
4. That silver necklace is cheap. _____
5. I like those wooden handicrafts over there. _____

¿Recuerdas?

Family & Classroom Objects

- Review the terms for family members.

los abuelos *(grandparents)*	**la abuela** *(grandmother)*	**el abuelo** *(grandfather)*
los padres *(parents)*	**la madre** *(mother)*	**el padre** *(father)*
los hijos *(children)*	**la hija** *(daughter)*	**el hijo** *(son)*
los tíos *(aunts and uncles)*	**la tía** *(aunt)*	**el tío** *(uncle)*
los primos *(cousins)*	**la prima** *(female cousin)*	**el primo** *(male cousin)*

- Review this list of classroom objects.

el pizarrón *(chalkboard)*	**la tiza** *(chalk)*	**el borrador** *(eraser)*
la ventana *(window)*	**el escritorio** *(desk)*	**el mapa** *(map)*
el reloj *(clock)*	**la silla** *(chair)*	**el cuaderno** *(notebook)*
el lápiz *(pencil)*	**la pluma** *(pen)*	**la calculadora** *(calculator)*
el examen *(test)*	**el papel** *(paper)*	

Práctica

Your whole family went shopping for school supplies. Follow the model to say what everyone bought for whom.

Modelo: mi madre / aquella silla / a mí *Mi madre me compró **aquella** silla a mí.*

1. mi tío / este lápiz / mi primo

   _____

2. mi padre / aquella calculadora / mi hermano

   _____

3. mi abuelo / este mapa / mi hermana

   _____

4. mi tía / este cuaderno / mi prima

   _____

5. mi madre / aquellas plumas / mis hermanos

   _____

6. mi abuela / ese papel / mí

   _____

7. mis tíos / aquellos escritorios / mis primos

   _____

8. mis padres / aquellas sillas / mis hermanas

   _____

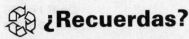 **¿Recuerdas?**

Level 1 pp. 441, 443
Level 1B pp. 264, 267

Numbers from 200 to 1,000,000

- Review how to count by hundreds. Remember that in Spanish, a period is used instead of a comma when separating numbers.

200	**doscientos**	700	**setecientos**
300	**trescientos**	800	**ochocientos**
400	**cuatrocientos**	900	**novecientos**
500	**quinientos**	1,000	**mil**
600	**seiscientos**	1,000,000	**un millón**

Gustar + infinitive

- Use **gustar** + **infinitive** to say what you and others like to do. Read the following sentences.

(A mí) **me gusta dar una caminata.**	*(I like to hike.)*
(A ti) **te gusta hacer surf de vela.**	*(You like to windsurf.)*
(A él/ella/usted) **le gusta acampar.**	*(He/she/it/you like to go camping.)*
(A nosotros(as)) **nos gusta caminar.**	*(We like to walk.)*
(A vosotros(as)) **os gusta ir de compras.**	*(You like to go shopping.)*
(A ellos(as)/ustedes) **les gusta montar a caballo.**	*(They/You like to ride horses.)*

Práctica

1 Explain what the following people like to do on weekends and how much each activity costs. Follow the model.

Modelo: Raúl / montar a caballo / $359

A Raúl le gusta montar a caballo. Cuesta trescientos cincuenta y nueve dólares.

1. tú / hacer surf de vela / $578 _____

_____

2. Teresa y yo / acampar / $299 _____

_____

3. ustedes / hacer surfing / $840 _____

_____

4. Paula y Elena / hacer una parrillada / $210 _____

_____

5. mi tía / comprar un anillo de oro / $1,399 _____

_____

UNIDAD 8 Lección 2

Reteaching and Practice

¿Recuerdas?

Level 1 p. 445
Level 1B p. 269

Present progressive

- The present progressive tense in Spanish is used to talk about what is happening right now. You use the present tense of **estar** + *present participle* (or **gerundio**) to form the present progressive. Read the following examples.

Estoy comprando un regalo.	*(I am buying a gift.)*
¿Qué **estás comiendo**?	*(What are you eating?)*
Ellos **están compartiendo** una pizza.	*(They are sharing a pizza.)*

Práctica

1 Tell what each person is doing at the market. Follow the model.

Modelo: Mis amigos / comer

Mis amigos están comiendo.

1. Elena / comprar un anillo _____

2. ellos / mirar las joyas _____

3. nosotros / regatear _____

4. el vendedor / ofrecer el recuerdo _____

5. Raúl / beber un refresco _____

6. ustedes / hablar con Luisa _____

7. tú / buscar unos aretes _____

8. yo / leer los anuncios _____

2 How different are your weekdays from your weekends? Write six sentences in the present progressive describing what you usually are doing at the following times during the week (**durante la semana**) and on Saturdays (**los sábados**).

	durante la semana	los sábados
1. A las siete de la mañana,		
2. A las dos de la tarde,		
3. A las ocho de la noche,		
4. A las doce de la noche,		

Did You Get It? Answer Key

PRÁCTICA DE VOCABULARIO
DAILY ROUTINES, pp. 2–3

1
1. el champú
2. el jabón
3. el cepillo
4. el secador de pelo
5. el cepillo de dientes
6. la toalla

2
1. cepillarse los dientes
2. despertarse
3. secarse
4. peinarse
5. vestirse
6. dormirse

3
1. Mario y Luisa hacen un viaje a la ciudad en coche.
2. Los estudiantes hacen un viaje a España en barco.
3. Mi familia y yo hacemos un viaje al campo en tren.

4
1. el jabón
2. el cepillo de dientes / la pasta de dientes
3. el champú
4. la toalla / el secador de pelo
5. el peine
6. la toalla

5
1. la cara
2. los dientes
3. champú
4. maquillarse
5. acostarse
6. la toalla
7. Normalmente
8. jabón

6
1. L
2. I
3. L
4. I
5. L
6. I

7 Answers will vary.

PRÁCTICA DE GRAMÁTICA
REFLEXIVE VERBS, p. 5

1
1. se
2. nos
3. te
4. se
5. se
6. se
7. nos
8. se
9. se
10. nos

2
1. Usted se pone la chaqueta nueva.
2. Vanesa y tú se cepillan muy rápido los dientes.
3. Silvia se pone un vestido elegante.
4. Ana y su hermana se maquillan demasiado.
5. Yo me lavo la cara todas las mañanas.
6. Mi hermana y yo nos acostamos temprano.

Did You Get It? Answer Key

3

1. María quiere levantarse a las ocho.
2. Tú quieres acostarte temprano.
3. Lisa y yo queremos maquillarnos antes de salir.
4. Paco quiere afeitarse antes de ir a la fiesta.
5. Marielsa y tú quieren despertarse tarde.

4

1. Ustedes se quieren cepillar los dientes después de comer.
2. Usted se quiere bañar en la mañana.
3. Tú te quieres despertar a las ocho mañana.
4. Nosotras nos queremos maquillar antes de salir.

5

1. José Antonio se lava las manos. Arturo lava su coche.
2. Andrea se pone la chaqueta. Luisa pone el plato en la mesa.
3. Tomeu duerme en el coche. Alison se duerme a las diez.

PRÁCTICA DE GRAMÁTICA
PRESENT PROGRESSIVE, p. 8

1

1. caminando
2. despertando
3. afeitando
4. maquillando
5. bañando
6. lavando
7. corriendo
8. durmiendo
9. trayendo
10. haciendo
11. diciendo
12. bebiendo

2

1. haciendo
2. tomando
3. comiendo
4. subiendo
5. jugando
6. bebiendo
7. trayendo
8. viendo

3

1. No, nos estamos cepillando los dientes.
2. No, me estoy maquillando.
3. No, se están despertando.
4. No, te estás poniendo mucho maquillaje.
5. No, se está peinando.

4

1. El chico está nadando.
2. Mi padre se está afeitando.
3. Mi amiga se está despertando.
4. José y Lupe están haciendo un viaje en tren.
5. La señora López está planchando la ropa.
6. Las chicas están tomando el sol.

5 Answers will vary.

Did You Get It? Answer Key

❀ ¿RECUERDAS?

PRETERITE OF **HACER**, CHORES, TELLING TIME, p. 10

1. Yo hice un viaje en tren a las siete y media.
2. Ana hizo la cama a las once menos veinte.
3. Tú hiciste la tarea a las seis y veinte.
4. Nosotros barremos el suelo de la cocina a las cuatro y diez.
5. Miraste la televisión en la sala a las nueve.
6. Limpió el baño a las siete y cuarto.

❀ ¿RECUERDAS?

DIRECT OBJECT PRONOUNS, p. 11

1. *la*
2. lo
3. lo
4. las
5. lo
6. nos
7. los
8. lo
9. te
10. me

1. Sí, lo llevó.
2. Sí, lo llevó.
3. Sí, la llevó.
4. Sí, la llevó.
5. Sí, las llevó.
6. Sí, lo llevó.
7. Sí, lo llevó.
8. Sí, los llevó.

❀ ¿RECUERDAS?

PARTS OF THE BODY, p. 12

1. la nariz
2. la cabeza
3. la boca
4. las piernas
5. los ojos
6. la mano

2

1. José se está lavando el brazo.
2. Tú te estás lavando el pelo.
3. Yo me estoy lavando los pies.
4. Aldo y yo nos estamos lavando las manos.

Did You Get It? Answer Key

PRÁCTICA DE VOCABULARIO

VACATION ACTIVITIES, pp. 14–15

❶

1. Tú compras una cerámica.
2. Mi padre compra un anillo de oro / de plata.
3. Yo compro unos aretes de oro / de plata.
4. Mis amigos compran un collar de madera.

❷

Alicia: Buenos días. **Quisiera** comprar un regalo para una amiga. ¿Puedo ver los aretes **de plata**, por favor?

Vendedor: Sí, claro. Son muy bonitos y de muy buena **calidad**.

Alicia: ¿Cuánto cuestan?

Vendedor: Diez mil quinientos colones.

Alicia: ¡Diez mil quinientos! ¡Es **demasiado**! Tengo ocho mil. ¿Tiene algo más **barato**?

Vendedor: Sí, el **collar** de madera cuesta ocho mil.

Alicia: También es bonito. Lo compro.

❸

1. orejas
2. cerámica
3. dedo
4. joyas / collares
5. recuerdos
6. mercado
7. calidad
8. regatear

❹

1. Los chicos acampan.
2. Mi hermana hace surf de vela.
3. Los amigos montan a caballo.
4. Mis padres hacen una parrillada.
5. Ustedes dan una caminata.

❺ Answers will vary.

PRÁCTICA DE GRAMÁTICA

INDIRECT OBJECT PRONOUNS, pp. 17–18

❶

1. me
2. le
3. te / le
4. nos
5. les

❷

1. me
2. nos
3. le
4. te
5. les
6. le
7. les
8. me

❸

1. Ustedes les van a comprar un regalo.
2. ¿Le vas a comprar los aretes para su cumpleaños?
3. Nos vas a comprar el DVD para la fiesta.
4. No te quiero comprar el collar en el mercado.
5. Óscar me va a comprar un anillo de plata para mi cumpleaños.

Did You Get It? Answer Key

4

Ariana: Hola, Enrique. Acabo de volver de mis vacaciones en la República Dominicana.

Enrique: ¿Qué tal el viaje? ¿Te gustó? ¿Y a nosotros, **nos** trajiste muchos recuerdos?

Ariana: Sí, **les** compré recuerdos a todos. **Le** compré un anillo de plata a Susana. **Les** compré unos collares de madera a Lupe y a Luisa. **Le** compré un artículo de madera a Jorge...

Enrique: Y a mí, ¿qué **me** compraste?

Ariana: A ti **te** compré el mejor regalo de todo.

5

1. María le compró aretes a su madre.
2. Tú me compraste un anillo a mí.
3. Lucía y yo les compramos artículos de cerámica a nuestros amigos.
4. Ustedes nos compraron unos collares a nosotras.
5. Paco te compró un DVD a ti.
6. Marielsa y tú le compraron un disco compacto a su primo.
7. Nosotros les compramos un regalo a ellos.

6

1. Tú le compraste un anillo.
2. Les compramos DVDs.
3. Te compré un collar de plata.
4. ¿Nos compraron recuerdos de su viaje?
5. Ustedes les compraron regalos a sus amigos.

PRÁCTICA DE GRAMÁTICA

DEMONSTRATIVE ADJECTIVES, pp. 20–21

1

1. **esta** joya; **este** arete de oro; **esta** camiseta; **este** mercado; **esta** artesanía; **este** artículo de madera
2. **esa** camisa; **ese** collar de madera; **ese** arete; **ese** anillo de plata; **ese** recuerdo; **esa** artesanía de metal
3. **aquel** anillo de oro; **aquel** recuerdo; **aquel** mercado de artesanías; **aquella** camisa roja; **aquel** collar de oro; **aquella** joya
4. **estas** camisas azules; **estas** faldas cortas; **estos** aretes de plata; **estos** mercados; **estos** artículos de madera; **estas** artesanías baratas
5. **esos** collares rojos; **esos** mercados; **esas** chaquetas cortas; **esos** recuerdos; **esos** sombreros marrones; **esos** artículos
6. **aquellas** camisetas blancas; **aquellos** anillos de plata; **aquellas** joyas baratas; **aquellos** artículos de madera; **aquellos** pantalones cortos; **aquellos** mercados

2

Olivia: **Esas** joyas son bonitas. ¿Puedo ver **aquel** anillo?

Vendedor: ¡Claro que sí! Es barato. Cuesta veinte mil colones.

Olivia: ¿Veinte mil colones? Es muy caro. ¿Y **estos** aretes de aquí? ¿Cuánto cuestan?

Vendedor: Son más baratos. Cuestan diez mil colones.

Olivia: Los aretes son caros también. ¿Y **ese** collar? ¡Tiene que ser barato!

Did You Get It? Answer Key

Vendedor: Sí, es la más barata de todas las joyas.

Olivia: Está bien. Compro **ese** collar.

❸

1. Aquellas chaquetas son bonitas.
2. Esos mercados venden joyas bonitas.
3. Estas artesanías son demasiado caras.
4. ¿Compro este collar de oro?
5. Aquel recuerdo es barato.

❹

1. This hike tired me a lot.
2. Those souvenirs are of good quality.
3. Is this handicraft made of gold or silver?
4. Those jewels over there cost too much.
5. Should I buy this ring or those earrings over there?

❺

1. Este mercado vende muchos recuerdos.
2. Esos aretes cuestan demasiado.
3. ¿Cuánto cuesta aquel anillo?
4. Ese collar de plata es barato.
5. Me gustan aquellas artesanías de madera.

¿RECUERDAS?
FAMILY AND CLASSROOM OBJECTS, p. 22

1. Mi tío le compró este lápiz a mi primo.
2. Mi padre le compró aquella calculadora a mi hermano.
3. Mi abuelo le compró este mapa a mi hermana.
4. Mi tía le compró este cuaderno a mi prima.
5. Mi madre les compró aquellas plumas a mis hermanos.
6. Mi abuela me compró ese papel a mí.
7. Mis tíos les compraron aquellos escritorios a mis primos.

8. Mis padres les compraron aquellas sillas a mis hermanas.

¿RECUERDAS?
NUMBERS FROM 200 TO 1,000,000, p. 23

1. A ti te gusta hacer surf de vela. Cuesta quinientos setenta y ocho dólares.
2. A nosotros nos gusta acampar. Cuesta doscientos noventa y nueve dólares.
3. A ustedes les gusta hacer surfing. Cuesta ochocientos cuarenta dólares.
4. A ellas les gusta hacer una parrillada. Cuesta doscientos diez dólares.
5. A ella le gusta comprar un anillo de oro. El anillo cuesta mil trescientos noventa y nueve dólares.

¿RECUERDAS?
PRESENT PROGRESSIVE, p. 24

❶

1. Elena está comprando un anillo.
2. Ellos están mirando las joyas.
3. Nosotros estamos regateando.
4. El vendedor está ofreciendo el recuerdo.
5. Raul está bebiendo un refresco.
6. Ustedes están hablando con Luisa.
7. Tú estás buscando unos aretes.
8. Yo estoy leyendo los anuncios.

❷ Answers will vary.

¡Lotería! *Práctica de vocabulario*

Play this game alone or with a friend. Take turns calling out the names of the items below. Use beans or coins to mark your answers. The first player with markers across three squares (horizontally, diagonally or vertically) wins.

 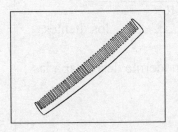 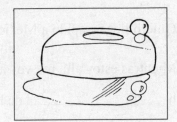

 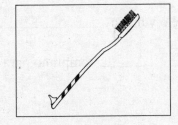 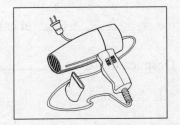

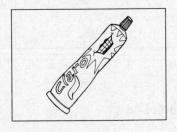 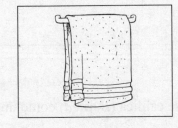 

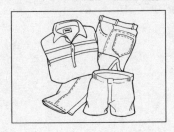  

1. el champú
2. la toalla
3. el cepillo
4. la pasta
5. el cepillo de dientes
6. la ducha
7. el peine
8. la secadora
9. el espejo
10. el jabón
11. la ropa
12. el reloj

Mi viaje *Vocabulario en contexto*

Complete the sentences about Jorge's trip to Mexico. Then use the code numbers under the letters to answer the question below.

1. Quiero llegar rápido a México. Voy a hacer un viaje en a ____ ____ ____ ____ .
                                                                          3

2. Mientras estoy allí, me voy a q ____ ____ ____ ____ ____ en un
                                          5

   h ____ ____ ____ ____ de lujo (*luxury*).
        7

3. Mi r ____ ____ ____ ____ ____ es siempre igual: me b ____ ____ ____ ,
              2   10

   me s ____ ____ ____ el cabello y me c ____ ____ ____ ____ ____ los dientes.
          6   1   9

4. Después me d ____ ____ ____ ____ ____ temprano para poderme despertar a las
                      8

   seis de la mañana.

5. Mañana iré al c ____ ____ ____ ____ a visitar mis abuelos.
                        4

Un hotel que es muy bueno se califica (*is rated*) como un hotel de...

____ ____ ____ ____ ____ ____ ____ ____ ____ ____ ____ ____ ____
 1   2   3   1   4   5   6   7   8   5   9   10 6

Rutina de reflexivos *Práctica de gramática 1*

Use the correct reflexive verb to complete the sentences and fill in the crossword puzzle.

Horizontal (*across*)

1. Para estar guapa, voy a _____ los ojos antes de la fiesta.

3. Javier y yo siempre necesitamos _____ después de un partido.

5. No me gusta ducharme en la noche—prefiero _____ .

Abajo (*down*)

2. Mamá tiene que _____ de la cama a las cinco para ir al trabajo.

4. Vosotros debéis _____ con mucha ropa para no tener frío.

6. Antes de un examen es importante _____ temprano.

7. Debes _____ el pelo antes de salir.

La rutina de Juan *Gramática en contexto*

Juan follows a logical daily routine. Fill in the blanks with the correct form of reflexive verbs to show how Juan is getting ready this morning. Then write the appropriate letters in the blanks of the secret message to find out what Juan forgets to do!

Primero, a las siete, Juan __ __   __ __ __ __ __ __ __ __ .
                                                          6

A las siete y cuarto, Juan __ __   __ __ __ __ __ __ __ .
                                                      4

Luego, le gusta __ __ __ __ __ __ __ __ rápidamente.
                              2

Cuando sale del baño, va por su ropa y __ __   __ __ __ · __ __ .
                                                             3

Entonces Juan baja a la cocina para desayunar.

Después del desayuno, él sube otra vez para __ __ __ __ __ __ los dientes.
                                                        5   7

¡Ya son las ocho! Juan tiene que __ __ __ __ __ __ la chaqueta y salir para la
                                   1   8
escuela.

What does Juan forget to do? __ __ __ __ __ __ __ __ .
                              1 2 3 4 5 6 7 8

34

Unidad 8, Lección 1
Practice Games

¡**Avancemos! 1**
Unit Resource Book

UNIDAD 8 Lección 1

Practice Games

Reverse Tic-Tac-Toe *Práctica de gramática 2*

Alone or with a friend, take turns finding the sentences that go with the present progressive verbs to see who wins at Tic-Tac-Toe. Place an X on the board over the correct answer for number 1. Then allow a partner to place an O over number 2. Play until one letter appears three times in a row on the board.

<u>X</u>	<u>O</u>
1. estamos llamando	**2.** estoy secándome
3. estáis vistiéndose	**4.** están cepillándose
5. estoy estudiando	**6.** estás comiendo
7. está peinándose	**8.** estamos decorando

____ ____ porque tengo un examen mañana.	____ ____ el piso porque está sucio.	La señora Lara ____ ____ el cabello.
Acabo de salir de bañarme, ____ ____ con la toalla.	Los niños ____ ____ los dientes.	____ ____ el salón para la fiesta.
____ ____ a Chile porque queremos hablar con nuestros tíos.	Tú ____ ____ una ensalada de pollo.	Eva y tú ____ ____ con su nueva ropa.

Who won? ____

Palabras escondidas (*Hidden words*) *Todo junto*

Unscramble the words associated with personal hygiene.

1. astap ___ ___ ___ ___ ___

2. njbóa ___ ___ ___ ___ ___

3. oaallt ___ ___ ___ ___ ___ ___

4. múchap ___ ___ ___ ___ ___ ___

5. eepni ___ ___ ___ ___ ___

6. draceso ___ ___ ___ ___ ___ ___ ___

7. llocpie ___ ___ ___ ___ ___ ___ ___

La rutina *Lectura*

The Martínez family is trying to get ready for school and work. Help the family by combining the phrases below to form sentences on the lines.

se levanta.

A las siete en la mañana, Nita

te pones el abrigo.

me visto.

Cuando hace frío, tú

Después de la ducha, yo

se despiertan a las siete y cuarto.

Mateo y Nicolás

Cuando nuestro pelo está mojado, Paloma y yo

nos secamos.

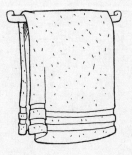

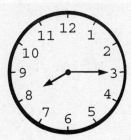

_____

_____

_____

_____

El alfabeto: A a Z *Repaso de la lección*

Use the letters of the alphabet to complete these nine words from the **Vocabulario**.
Use each letter only once.

A B C D E F G H I J L M N Ñ O P Q R S T U V

1. ___ u e ___ a r ___ e
2. ___ i a ___ e
3. ___ ___ a m p ___
4. ___ a ___ a r s e
5. a ___ e ___ ___ a r s e
6. ___ e i ___ ___ e
7. t ___ a ___ l ___
8. ___ e n e ___ a l ___ e n t ___

UNIDAD 8 Lección 1

Practice Games

Vamos a Costa Rica *Práctica de vocabulario*

Play the board game by unscrambling the following activities that you can do while on vacation in Costa Rica. Once you have unscrambled each activity, go to that activity's spot on the board. The player who gets to home base first wins.

1. En la Playa Naranjo puedes practicar este deporte que es muy divertido, pero también un poco peligroso (*dangerous*).

   creha rfus ed leva _____

2. En Puerto Viejo puedes disfrutar del paisaje (*landscape*) cuando haces esto.

   rad nau mnaataci _____

3. En Guanacaste puedes hacer esto y pasearte con este animal.

   rmnota a llaacob _____

4. Si te encanta ir al mercado, puedes hacer esto cuando visites a Sarchí.

   rrapmoc sodreucer _____

5. Mucha gente va al Parque Nacional Cahuita para hacer esto con la familia.

   rapmaca _____

6. También pueden hacer esto en el Parque Nacional Cahuita cuando tienen hambre.

   rehac anu rrillpaad _____

Centro comercial	Parque Nacional Cahuita		Sarchí	Parque de diversión	Feria
	Costa Rica				Guanacaste
Puerto Viejo					Acuario
Hotel					Parque Nacional Cahuita
Casa	Zoológico	Playa Naranjo		Museo	Restaurante Mercado

Oraciones tuyas *Vocabulario en contexto*

Use the words in the word bank to create five sentences. Try to use as many of the words in each sentence as possible. Score each sentence as follows:

2 words from the word bank: 4 points

3 words: 8 points

4 words: 10 points

5 words: 12 points

6 words: 14 points

If possible, compare scores with a partner.

caro	plata	collar	mercado	caminata	montaña rusa
acuario	feria	miedo	anillo	arete	museo
aire	acampar	madera		parque de diversiones	

1. _____

_____

_____

2. _____

_____

_____

3. _____

_____

_____

4. _____

_____

_____

5. _____

_____

_____

UNIDAD 8 Lección 2

Practice Games

Rimas *Práctica de gramática 1*

Indirect objects state to whom or for whom the action of the verb is intended.
Read the following rhymes and circle each indirect object noun. Then underline the
indirect object pronoun.

A Ana le gustan las joyas.
Yo le compré algo de oro,
el problema es que,
¡es un gorro!

A nosotros nos gusta la parrillada.
Después mi madre está cansada.
A ti mi padre te ofrece una ensalada
¡no entiende porque estás enfadada!

Para mi madre mi padre cocina la sopa.
Y siempre le plancha la ropa.
Pero a mí mi padre me invita,
¡a comer una pizza!

Esmeralda tiene regalos *Gramática en contexto*

Esmeralda is shopping for gifts for her family. Cross off the appropriate indirect object pronoun in the box to indicate for whom she has found a gift. One person will not have an indirect object pronoun in the box.

Who couldn't Esmeralda find a gift for? _____

para nosotros: tres discos compactos

para Mamá: un collar de oro

para Juan y Diego: un bate

para mí: unos aretes de oro

para vosotros: camisetas

para Lucia: un vestido

para ti: un anillo de plata

para la maestra: un artículo de madera

para Sandi y Juana: cerámica

Ya _____ tengo un regalo para...			
te	le	os	le
les	nos	nos	os
les	le	te	le

Después de comprar *Práctica de gramática 2*

Raúl's souvenirs are a mess in his suitcase. Help him sort them out according to which demonstrative adjective he should use for each. Remember that demonstrative adjectives must agree in number and gender with the noun they modify.

este	aquellos	esa	estas
_____	_____	_____	_____
_____	_____	_____	
_____	_____		
	_____		

anillo	alfombras	camisa	collares
	espejo	gorros	jeans
radio		silla	sombreros

UNIDAD 8 Lección 2   Practice Games

Adjetivos escondidos *Todo junto*

Find the word from **Vocabulario** hidden in each sentence that describes things you can buy in a market. Hint: you will have to look in all the words to find each answer.

1. cantaron   ____ ____ ____ ____

2. decoraron   ____ ____ ____ ____ ____

3. barro tanto (*so much*)   ____ ____ ____ ____ ____ ____

4. patino delante   ____ ____ ____ ____ ____ ____ ____

5. dibujaron mujeres altas   ____ ____ ____ ____ ____ ____ ____ ____

6. buscan la ciudad vieja   ____ ____ ____ ____ ____ ____ ____ ____ ____ ____ ____ ____

Tic-Tac-Toe *Lectura cultural*

Alone or taking turns with a friend, find the correct demonstrative adjectives in the boxes to see who wins at Tic-Tac-Toe. Place an X on the board over the correct answer for number 1. Then allow a partner to place an O over number 2. Play until one of the letters has won.

X	**O**
1. Yo quiero _____ (*this*) vestido.	**2.** No necesito _____ (*that*) anillo.
3. ¿Ves _____ (*that one over there*) collar?	**4.** Usaste _____ (*that*) raqueta.
5. Compré _____ (*these*) globos.	**6.** ¿Te gusta _____ (*that one over there*) cama?
7. Nesecitan _____ (*those*) cepillos.	**8.** ¿Como _____ (*these*) patatas?

ese	aquellas	aquel
aquella	esos	esa
estas	estos	este

Who won? _____

Copyright © by McDougal Littell, a division of Houghton Mifflin Company.

UNIDAD 8 Lección 2   **Practice Games**

A vacaciones *Repaso de la lección*

Help Rosita decide what to do on her vacation by matching the brochures to the activities they describe.

Cocina sobre fuego al aire libre. Duerme debajo de las estrellas.	Tenemos todas las joyas que puedes imaginar.	¿Te gustan los animales? Camina con un animal simpático.	Si te gusta el mar, te va a gustar esa aventura.

montar a caballo	hacer surf de vela	acampar	ir al mercado

Practice Games Answer Key

PAGE 32
Vocabulario en contexto

1. avión
2. quedar, hotel
3. rutina, baño, seco, cepillo
4. duermo
5. campo

cinco estrellas

PAGE 33
Práctica de gramática 1

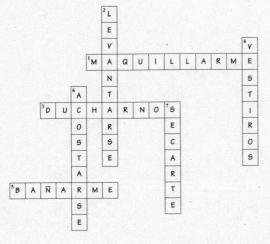

PAGE 34
Gramática en contexto

se despierta
se levanta
ducharse
se viste
lavarse
ponerse

PEINARSE

PAGE 35
Práctica de gramática 2

X	X	X
Estoy estudiando porque tengo un examen mañana.	___ ___ el piso porque está sucio.	La señora Lara está peinándose el cabello.
O	*O*	*O*
Acabo de salir de bañarme, estoy secándome con la toalla.	Los niños están cepillándose los dientes.	Estamos decorando el salón para la fiesta.
X	*O*	X
Estamos llamando a Chile porque queremos hablar con nuestros tíos.	Tú estás comiendo una ensalada de pollo.	Eva y tú están vistiendose con su nueva ropa.

O wins.

Practice Games Answer Key

PAGE 36

Todo junto

1. pasta
2. jabón
3. toalla
4. champú
5. peine
6. secador
7. cepillo

PAGE 37

Lectura

Cuando hace frío, tú te pones el abrigo.

A las siete en la mañana, Nita se levanta.

Después de la ducha, yo me visto.

Mateo y Nicolás se despiertan a las siete y cuarto.

Cuando nuestro pelo está mojado, Paloma y yo nos secamos.

PAGE 38

Repaso de la lección

1. quedarse
2. viaje
3. champú
4. bañarse
5. afeitarse
6. peine
7. toalla
8. generalmente

Practice Games Answer Key

Copyright © by McDougal Littell, a division of Houghton Mifflin Company.

PAGE 39
Práctica de vocabulario

1. hacer surf de vela
2. dar una caminata
3. montar a caballo
4. comprar recuerdos
5. acampar
6. hacer una parrillada

PAGE 40
Vocabulario en contexto

Answers will vary.

PAGE 41
Práctica de gramática 1

(A Ana) le gustan las joyas.
Yo le compré algo de oro,
el problema es que,
¡es un gorro!

(A nosotros) nos gusta la parrillada.
Después mi madre está cansada.
(A ti) mi padre te ofrece una ensalada
¡no entiende porque estás enfadada!

Para (mi madre) mi padre cocina la sopa.
Y siempre le plancha la ropa.
Pero (a mí) mi padre me invita,
¡a comer una pizza!

PAGE 42
Gramática en contexto

For herself, "para mí", there is no "me" in the box.

Ya _____ tengo un regalo para...			
te	le	os	le
les	nos	nos	os
les	les	te	le

PAGE 43
Práctica de gramática 2

este: anillo, espejo, radio
aquellos: gorros, collares, sombreros, jeans
esa: silla, camisa
estas: alfombras

PAGE 44
Todo junto

1. caro
2. de oro
3. barato
4. de plata
5. de madera
6. buena calidad

Practice Games Answer Key

PAGE 45

Lectura cultural

O ese	aquellas	X aquel
O aquella	X esos	O esa
O estas	X estos	X este

O wins.

PAGE 46

Repaso de la lección

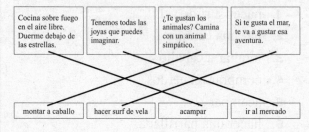

Video Activities *Vocabulario*

PRE-VIEWING ACTIVITY

Before you view the film, answer these questions about your morning routine.

1 What time do you get up in the morning on school days?

_____

_____

2 What do you do in the morning to get ready for school?

_____

_____

3 What are some household items you use in the morning?

_____

_____

4 What time do you leave for school?

_____

_____

VIEWING ACTIVITY

Read the following list of activities before watching the video. While you watch, indicate with a checkmark (☐) which character does each of these activities in the morning.

Susana	Jorge	
_____	_____	**1.** afeitarse la cara
_____	_____	**2.** bañarse rápidamente
_____	_____	**3.** ducharse
_____	_____	**4.** lavarse la cara
_____	_____	**5.** levantarse a las siete
_____	_____	**6.** peinarse
_____	_____	**7.** levantarse a las siete y media
_____	_____	**8.** lavarse el pelo
_____	_____	**9.** secarse el pelo por quince minutos

Video Activities *Vocabulario*

POST-VIEWING ACTIVITY

After you watch the video, circle the best answer to each multiple-choice question.

1. Susana se levanta a las _____.
   a. siete
   b. siete y cuarto
   c. siete y media

2. Antes de las siete y veinte, Susana _____.
   a. se lava su pelo
   b. se afeita su cara
   c. se cepilla sus dientes

3. Susana cumple su rutina a las _____.
   a. siete y media
   b. siete treinta y cinco
   c. ocho y media

4. A las siete, Jorge se _____.
   a. baña
   b. levanta
   c. despierta

5. Después de ducharse, Jorge _____ por quince minutos.
   a. se lava la cara
   b. se seca el pelo
   c. se cepilla los dientes

6. El papá de Jorge y Susana no puede secarse sin su _____.
   a. toalla
   b. jabón
   c. peine

UNIDAD 8 Lección 1

Video Activities

Video Activities *Telehistoria escena 1*

PRE-VIEWING ACTIVITY

Answer the following questions about your ideal vacation.

1 Where would you go on your ideal vacation?

_____

_____

2 How would you get there?

_____

_____

3 With whom would you go?

_____

_____

4 What would you do while on vacation?

_____

_____

5 How long would your vacation be?

_____

_____

VIEWING ACTIVITY

Read the statements below before watching the video. Then, while you watch the video, check off (🕐) the statements that Susana says.

_____ Necesito tomar unas buenas vacaciones.

_____ Voy a hacer un viaje con toda la familia.

_____ Me gustaría ir en avión o en tren.

_____ ¿Voy al campo o a la ciudad?

_____ El año pasado mi familia y yo fuimos al campo.

_____ Mi hermano es imposible.

_____ Quiero quedarme en casa.

Video Activities *Telehistoria escena 1*

POST-VIEWING ACTIVITY

Choose the word or phrase that best completes each sentence.

1. Susana necesita tomar vacaciones lejos de su _____.
   a. hermano
   b. papá
   c. mamá

2. Ella y su familia pueden ir en _____.
   a. avión o en tren
   b. avión o en barco
   c. avión o en coche

3. _____ de Susana quiere saber lo que ella hace.
   a. El padre
   b. La madre
   c. El hermano

4. El año pasado Susuana y su familia fueron _____.
   a. al campo
   b. a la playa
   c. a la ciudad

5. Susana prefiere ir _____.
   a. al campo
   b. a la playa
   c. a la ciudad

6. Jorge quiere saber dónde está _____.
   a. el agua
   b. la leche
   c. el jugo de naranja

7. Susana va a quedarse en _____.
   a. la casa
   b. la sala
   c. un hotel

Video Activities

UNIDAD 8 Lección 1

Video Activities *Telehistoria escena 2*

PRE-VIEWING ACTIVITY

Answer the following questions about your daily routine.

1 What do you do every morning to get ready for school?

_____

_____

2 How long does it take you to do all of these things?

_____

_____

3 Do you have to share the bathroom with anyone?

_____

_____

4 Do other people in your house ever make it difficult for you to get ready on time?

_____

_____

VIEWING ACTIVITY

Read the following list of activities before watching the video. Then, while you watch the video, check off (⏱) each activity that Jorge has to do in order to be on time.

_____	acostarse a las diez	_____	cepillarse los dientes
_____	acostarse a las ocho	_____	afeitarse
_____	ducharse	_____	secarse el pelo
_____	lavarse la cara	_____	dormirse
_____	lavarse el pelo	_____	maquillarse
_____	levantarse a la siete	_____	peinarse
_____	levantarse a las seis	_____	ponerse la ropa

Video Activities *Telehistoria escena 2*

POST-VIEWING ACTIVITY

Complete each sentence with the appropriate phrase.

1. La madre de ellos está ____   a. se levanta temprano.

2. Susana y Jorge están ____.   b. no le gusta levantarse temprano.

3. El sábado Susana y Jorge quieren ____.   c. en la oficina.

4. Ellos tienen que tomar ____.   d. trabajar el sábado.

5. El primer autobús sale ____.   e. para ir a la escuela.

6. Cuando Jorge está de vacaciones ____.   f. a las nueve de la mañana.

7. Cuando Jorge está en la escuela ____.   g. ir a la playa.

8. Jorge se viste rápidamente ____.   h. de vacaciones.

9. El papá de ellos tiene que ____.   i. el autobús a la playa.

UNIDAD 8 Lección 1

Video Activities

Unidad 8, Lección 1
Video Activities

56

¡Avancemos! 1
Unit Resource Book

Video Activities *Telehistoria escena 3*

PRE-VIEWING ACTIVITY

Answer the following questions.

1. Do you have any brothers or sisters? If so, how old are they?

_____

_____

2. What do you think is an advantage to having siblings?

_____

_____

3. What do you think is a disadvantage to having siblings?

_____

_____

4. Would you rather have an older sibling or a younger sibling? Why?

_____

_____

VIEWING ACTIVITY

Read the following list of activities before watching the video. While you watch the video, indicate with a checkmark (🕐) whether Susana, Jorge, or **el papá** is doing each activity.

Susana	Jorge	el papá	
_____	_____	_____	Está comiendo mucho.
_____	_____	_____	Está preparando la comida.
_____	_____	_____	Está bebiendo algo.
_____	_____	_____	Está esperando.
_____	_____	_____	Está escuchando música.
_____	_____	_____	Está poniendo un sándwich en la mochila.
_____	_____	_____	Los está llamando a ellos.
_____	_____	_____	Está pensando lo que necesita.

Video Activities *Telehistoria escena 3*

POST-VIEWING ACTIVITY

Indicate whether each of the following sentences is true (**T**) or false (**F**).

1. Jorge tiene mucha hambre.　　　　　　　　　　　　T　　F

2. Jorge come la comida y bebe un jugo.　　　　　　　T　　F

3. Susana y Jorge necesitan salir rápidamente porque
   su padre los está esperando.　　　　　　　　　　　T　　F

4. Jorge está escuchando a su papá.　　　　　　　　　T　　F

5. Susana prepara un sándwich para su hermano.　　　T　　F

6. Susana y Jorge van al centro comercial.　　　　　　T　　F

7. Jorge sabe lo que necesita antes de salir de casa.　　T　　F

8. Su papá tiene que ir al centro comercial.　　　　　　T　　F

UNIDAD 8 Lección 1

Video Activities

58

Unidad 8, Lección 1
Video Activities

¡Avancemos! 1
Unit Resource Book

Video Activities *Vocabulario*

PRE-VIEWING ACTIVITY

Before you watch the video, answer these questions about vacations and shopping.

1. A friend is wondering where to go on vacation. Give your friend some suggestions.

_____

_____

2. What activities do you like to do on vacation?

_____

_____

3. What kinds of souvenirs do you like to buy?

_____

_____

4. What kinds of jewelry do you like to wear or see on other people?

_____

_____

VIEWING ACTIVITY

Before you watch the video, read all the activities below. Then, while you watch, indicate with a checkmark (☺) which activities Susana's friend suggests.

_____ **1.** acampar

_____ **2.** caminar en el parque

_____ **3.** ir al parque de diversiones

_____ **4.** dormir mucho

_____ **5.** ir a la playa

_____ **6.** montar a caballo

_____ **7.** visitar museos

_____ **8.** ir al mercado

_____ **9.** viajar a otro país

_____ **10.** ir a la biblioteca

Video Activities *Vocabulario*

POST-VIEWING ACTIVITY

After watching the film, use the words in the word bank to complete each sentence.

acampan	aire libre	aretes	barata	la playa	mercado	plata

1. Las chicas están comiendo al _____ .

2. Si las chicas _____ , pueden dormir debajo de las estrellas.

3. Las chicas pueden nadar si van a _____ .

4. Pueden ir de compras en el _____ .

5. Hay joyas como anillos y _____ .

6. Las joyas son de madera, oro y _____ .

7. Susana quiere una actividad _____ porque no tiene mucho dinero.

UNIDAD 8 Lección 2

Video Activities

Video Activities *Telehistoria escena 1*

PRE-VIEWING ACTIVITY

Answer the following questions about specialty shopping.

1 Have you ever been to an open–air market?

_____

_____

2 What types of items are sold at an open–air market?

_____

_____

3 What might be an advantage to shopping at an open–air market in comparison to a mall?

_____

_____

4 If you were looking for a bargain, would you shop at an open–air market or a mall? Explain your answer.

_____

_____

VIEWING ACTIVITY

Read the statements below before watching the video. Then complete the activity as you watch. Write **sí** (*yes*) next to the statements that Susana makes and **no** (*no*) next to the statements that she does not make.

_____ **1.** Papi, ¿por qué no compras un carro nuevo?

_____ **2.** ¡Viajar en taxi es divertido!

_____ **3.** A ver… ¿este anillo de oro?

_____ **4.** ¿Cuánto cuestan los collares de oro?

_____ **5.** Tengo diez colones, nada más.

_____ **6.** Estamos en un mercado. Aquí nos gusta regatear.

Video Activities *Telehistoria escena 1*

POST-VIEWING ACTIVITY

Choose the word(s) that best complete(s) each of the following sentences.

1. La amiga de Susana piensa que el carro de su papá es un _____.
   - **a.** taxi
   - **b.** tren
   - **c.** arete

2. Susana quiere ver el anillo de _____.
   - **a.** madera
   - **b.** plata
   - **c.** oro

3. El anillo cuesta _____ colones.
   - **a.** diez mil
   - **b.** veinte mil
   - **c.** veinte

4. Susana piensa que la joya es muy _____.
   - **a.** vieja
   - **b.** barata
   - **c.** cara

5. La vendedora no quiere _____ con Susana.
   - **a.** regatear
   - **b.** hablar
   - **c.** trabajar

UNIDAD 8 Lección 2

Video Activities

Video Activities *Telehistoria escena 2*

PRE-VIEWING ACTIVITY

Answer the following questions about window shopping.

1 How would you define a window–shopper?

_____

_____

2 Do you window–shop sometimes?

_____

_____

3 If so, what types of items do you look for when you window–shop?

_____

_____

4 Does window–shopping ever lead you to buy anything?

_____

_____

VIEWING ACTIVITY

Read the following statements before watching the video. While you watch the video indicate with a checkmark (⊙) whether Susana or **el vendedor** (*the salesman*) makes each statement. Hint: the statements are reworded.

Susana	el vendedor	
_____	_____	¿Me deja verla?
_____	_____	Y los aretes de plata, ¿le gustan a usted?
_____	_____	Es un poco cara, ¿no?
_____	_____	¿Cuánto cuesta esa joya?
_____	_____	¡Todo es muy caro!
_____	_____	Me gustan los collares de madera.

Video Activities *Telehistoria escena 2*

POST-VIEWING ACTIVITY

Complete each sentence with the appropriate phrase.

1. El vendedor quiere ayudar _____ .

2. Susana dice que _____ .

3. El vendedor le deja ver a Susana _____ .

4. El vendedor dice que _____ .

5. El collar de oro cuesta _____ .

6. Jorge le dice a Susana _____ .

7. Puede ser que _____ .

a. el collar de oro.

b. Trini Salgado está en la tienda.

c. que a Susana le gustan las cosas caras.

d. más de cuarenta mil colones.

e. todo en la tienda es caro.

f. a Susana y Jorge.

g. la joya es un poco cara.

Video Activities *Telehistoria escena 3*

PRE-VIEWING ACTIVITY

Answer the following questions.

1 In the last episode, Susana and Jorge see a girl wearing a soccer uniform enter the store. Who do you think this person might be? Explain your answer.

_____

_____

2 Based on your answer to the previous question, and what you already know about Susana and Jorge, write a short paragraph about what you think will happen in this episode.

_____

_____

_____

_____

VIEWING ACTIVITY

Read the following statements before watching the video. While you watch the video, indicate whether each statement is true (T) or false (F).

1.	El vendedor le quiere vender un artículo de madera a Susana y a Jorge.	T	F
2.	Los aretes de oro cuestan veinte mil colones.	T	F
3.	El collar de oro cuesta cuarenta y tres mil colones.	T	F
4.	Jorge y Susana ven a Trini Salgado.	T	F
5.	Trini compra una joya.	T	F
6.	Jorge no encuentra la camiseta en su mochila.	T	F
7.	Después de regatear con el vendedor, Trini sale de la tienda rápidamente.	T	F
8.	La mamá de Jorge lavó la camiseta de Alicia.	T	F

UNIDAD 8 Lección 2   Video Activities

Video Activities *Telehistoria escena 3*

POST-VIEWING ACTIVITY

Who is saying or doing what to whom? Choose the correct person or people to complete each sentence. Hint: one answer is used more than once.

1. El vendedor les pregunta _____ si a ellos les gustan las joyas.

    a. a Susana

2. Susana le dice _____ que la chica es Trini.

    b. a Jorge

3. Jorge le manda la camiseta _____ .

    c. a Susana y a Jorge

4. Susana le dice _____ que Trini compra unos aretes.

    d. al vendedor

5. Jorge y Susana no le escuchan _____ .

    e. a Alicia

6. Jorge le pregunta _____ qué está haciendo Trini.

7. Susana le dice _____ que Trini compra unos aretes.

UNIDAD 8 Lección 2

Video Activities

Video Activities Answer Key

VOCABULARIO, pp. 51–52

PRE-VIEWING ACTIVITY

1. Answers will vary. Possible answer: I get up at seven o'clock.
2. Answers will vary. Possible answer: I get dressed, comb my hair, and brush my teeth.
3. Answers will vary. Possible answer: I use a toothbrush, toothpaste, and comb.
4. Answers will vary. Possible answer: I leave at 7:45.

VIEWING ACTIVITY

1. Jorge
2. Susana
3. Jorge
4. Susana
5. Susana
6. Susana, Jorge
7. Jorge
8. Jorge
9. Jorge

POST-VIEWING ACTIVITY

1. a
2. c
3. b
4. c
5. b
6. a

TELEHISTORIA ESCENA 1, pp. 53–54

PRE-VIEWING ACTIVITY

1. Answers will vary. Possible answer: I would go to Alaska.
2. Answers will vary. Possible answer: I would take an airplane to Alaska.
3. Answers will vary. Possible answer: I would go with all of my best friends.
4. Answers will vary. Possible answer: I would go hiking, ice climbing, and dog-sledding.
5. Answers will vary. Possible answer: My vacation would be a month long.

VIEWING ACTIVITY

Marked items should be:

Necesito tomar unas buenas vacaciones. ⏲

¿Voy al campo o a la ciudad? ⏲

El año pasado mi familia y yo fuimos al campo. ⏲

Mi hermano es imposible. ⏲

POST-VIEWING ACTIVITY

1. a
2. b
3. c
4. a
5. c
6. b
7. c

TELEHISTORIA ESCENA 2, pp. 55–56

PRE-VIEWING ACTIVITY

1. Answers will vary. Possible answer: First I take a shower. Then I blow-dry my hair and put on my make-up. Then I get dressed and eat breakfast. Finally, before leaving the house, I brush my teeth.
2. Answers will vary. Possible answer: It takes me thirty minutes to do all of these things.
3. Answers will vary. Possible answer: Yes, I have to share the bathroom with my two sisters.
4. Answers will vary. Possible answer: Yes. Sometimes I am late for school because my sisters take too long in the bathroom.

VIEWING ACTIVITY

acostarse a las diez ⏲	cepillarse los dientes
acostarse a las ocho	afeitarse
ducharse ⏲	secarse el pelo ⏲
lavarse la cara	dormirse
lavarse el pelo ⏲	maquillarse
levantarse a las siete	peinarse ⏲
levantarse a las seis ⏲	ponerse la ropa ⏲

POST-VIEWING ACTIVITY

1. c
2. h
3. g
4. i
5. f
6. b
7. a
8. e
9. d

TELEHISTORIA ESCENA 3, pp. 57–58

PRE-VIEWING ACTIVITY

1. Answers will vary. Possible answer: Yes, I have two brothers. One is seventeen and the other is nineteen.
2. Answers will vary. Possible answer: There is always company around.
3. Answers will vary. Possible answer: They can order you around.
4. Answers will vary. Possible answer: I would rather have a younger sibling to look up to me.

VIEWING ACTIVITY

Está comiendo mucho: Jorge

Está bebiendo algo: Jorge

Está esperando: el papá

Está escuchando música: Jorge

Está poniendo un sándwich en la mochila: Susana

Está llamando a ellos: el papá

Está pensando de lo que necesita: Jorge

POST-VIEWING ACTIVITY

1. T
2. F
3. T
4. F
5. T
6. T
7. F
8. F

Video Activities Answer Key

VOCABULARIO, pp. 59–60

PRE-VIEWING ACTIVITY

1. Answers will vary. Possible answer: My friend could go to the beach or go camping.
2. Answers will vary. Possible answer: I like to surf, shop, or go horseback-riding.
3. Answers will vary. Possible answer: I like to buy T-shirts and jewelry.
4. Answers will vary. Possible answer: I like silver earrings.

VIEWING ACTIVITY

Marked items should be:

acampar

caminar en el parque

ir a la playa

montar a caballo

ir al mercado

POST-VIEWING ACTIVITY

1. aire libre
2. acampan
3. la playa
4. mercado
5. aretes
6. plata
7. barata

TELEHISTORIA ESCENA 1, pp. 61–62

PRE-VIEWING ACTIVITY

1. Answers will vary. Possible answer: Yes, I have been to an open-air market.
2. Answers will vary. Possible answer: You can find fruit, vegetables, arts and crafts, and jewelry at open-air markets.
3. Answers will vary. Possible answer: You can find original pieces of art at a market; you can enjoy the fresh air.
4. Answers will vary. Possible answer: I would shop at an open-air market because you can bargain with vendors. By bargaining you can sometimes get an item for much cheaper than the original ticket price.

VIEWING ACTIVITY

1.	sí	2.	no
3.	sí	4.	no
5.	no	6.	no

POST-VIEWING ACTIVITY

1.	a	2.	c
3.	b	4.	c
5.	a		

TELEHISTORIA ESCENA 2, pp. 63–64

PRE-VIEWING ACTIVITY

1. Answers will vary. Possible answer: A window shopper is a person who browses in a store but doesn't buy anything. He or she goes to a store simply to look at what there is to buy.
2. Answers will vary. Possible answer: Yes, I window shop.
3. Answers will vary. Possible answer: I like to window shop for really expensive items like stereo systems and television sets.
4. Answers will vary. Possible answer: Sometimes, if I see something I really like.

VIEWING ACTIVITY

¿Me deja verla? Susana

Y los aretes de plata, ¿le gustan a usted? el vendedor

Es un poco cara, ¿no? el vendedor

¿Cuánto cuesta esa joya? Susana

¡Todo es muy caro! Susana

Me gustan los collares de madera. Susana

POST-VIEWING ACTIVITY

1.	f	2.	e
3.	a	4.	g
5.	d	6.	c
7.	b		

TELEHISTORIA ESCENA 3, pp. 65–66

PRE-VIEWING ACTIVITY

1. Answers will vary. Possible answer: I think the girl is Trini Salgado because she is supposed to be at the shopping center that day.

2. Answers will vary. Possible answer: The girl who enters the store is Trini Salgado. Jorge recognizes her, but Susana doesn't believe that her brother knows what he is talking about. Jorge approaches Trini and asks her for an autograph. Trini already has a pen and is ready to sign his shirt, but when Jorge looks for Alicia's shirt he remembers that he left it in the kitchen at home. Trini already has a signed picture of herself in her backpack. She gives it to Jorge.

VIEWING ACTIVITY

1.	F	2.	T
3.	F	4.	T
5.	T	6.	T
7.	F	8.	T

POST-VIEWING ACTIVITY

1.	c	2.	b
3.	e	4.	b
5.	d	6.	a
7.	b		

Video Scripts

VOCABULARIO

Father: ¡Nuestros dos hijos son muy diferentes!

Mother: Pues, sí. La rutina de Susana: a las siete de la mañana, se levanta. Se lava la cara, se baña rápidamente. Se cepilla los dientes: son las siete y veinte. Se maquilla: son las siete y veinticinco. Se peina: son las siete y media. Se pone la ropa: ¡son las siete y treinta y cinco!

Mother: ¿Pero Jorge?

Father: ¡Uf! Su rutina normal es: se despierta a las siete, pero se levanta a las siete y media. Se ducha y se lava el pelo, se seca el pelo. Quince minutos y se peina. Luego, se afeita los cinco pelos de la cara, ¡diez minutos más! Son las ocho y treinta. Y, ¿dónde está?

Mother: ¡Ahora, tú!

Father: Si, pero... ¿Dónde está mi champú? ¿Mi pasta de dientes favorita? ¿Mi cepillo de dientes? ¿Mi jabón especial? Y, ¿mi peine? ¿Donde está? Mi toalla? El secador de pelo?

Mother: Las nueve y treinta y, ¿dónde está?

TELEHISTORIA ESCENA 1

Susana: ¡Ay, necesito tomar unas buenas vacaciones lejos de mi hermano! Voy a hacer un viaje con mi familia; podemos ir en avión, en barco...

Jorge: ¡Susana!

Susana: ¿Voy al campo o a la ciudad? El año pasado mi familia y yo fuimos al campo. Pero yo generalmente prefiero...

Jorge: ¡Susana! ¿Qué haces? Susana, ¿dónde está la leche?

Susana: ¡Mamá, papá!

Madre: Susana, ¿qué?

Susana: Mi hermano es imposible. ¡Me voy a quedar en un hotel!

Video Scripts

TELEHISTORIA ESCENA 2

Susana: ¿Y Mamá? ¿Dónde está?

Padre: En la oficina. Ahora ustedes tienen vacaciones, ¿no? ¿Qué planes tienen?

Jorge: Queremos ir a la playa el sábado. ¿Podemos?

Padre: Sí, pero el primer autobús a Playa Jacó sale a las 9. Con tu rutina, Jorge, debes acostarte a las diez, para levantarte a las seis de la mañana. Necesitas tiempo para ducharte, lavarte el pelo, secarte el pelo, peinarte, ponerte la ropa...

Jorge: ¿Despertarme a las seis? Normalmente me levanto temprano y me visto rápidamente para ir a la escuela, pero, ¡estoy de vacaciones! Papá, ¿podemos ir a la playa en carro?

Padre: No, tengo que ir a la oficina el sábado.

Jorge: ¿Puedo usar yo el carro?

TELEHISTORIA ESCENA 3

Susana: Jorge, ¡estás comiendo y comiendo, por favor! ¿Quieres ir al centro comercial o no? Papá nos está esperando, tiene que ir a la oficina. Jorge, ¿no me escuchas? ¡Nos está llamando Papá!

Jorge: Pero estoy comiendo el desayuno...

Susana: ¡Vamos, ahora! ¿No me estás escuchando? Papá está esperando. ¡Toma la mochila!

Jorge: Un momento, hay algo. Susana, espera. Necesito algo importante pero, ¿qué puede ser?

UNIDAD 8 Lección 1

Video Scripts

Video Scripts

VOCABULARIO

Susana: Estoy de vacaciones y, ¿qué hago? Comer al aire libre. Quisiera salir de la ciudad.

Andrea: ¿Qué te gusta hacer en tu tiempo libre, después de las clases o en vacaciones? ¿Acampar? ¿Hacer el surf de vela o el surfing? ¿Montar a caballo? ¿Le gustaría ir a la playa? Cuesta más o menos cincuenta mil colones.

Susana: ¡Ay, demasiado caro!

Andrea: ¿Algo más barato? También puede quedarse en la ciudad. Puede ir al mercado a comprar artesanías. Tienen muchos artículos de madera, de oro, de plata y cerámica; y joyas: collares, anillos, aretes...

Susana: No tengo mucho dinero.

Andrea: Mira, Susana, podemos dar caminatas en el parque de aquí o hacer una parrillada con los amigos.

Susana: Sí, pero...

Andrea: ¿Qué?

Susana: Mi hermano. Tengo que volver a casa con mi hermano.

Andrea: ¡Ah, no! Yo puedo ayudar con las vacaciones, pero con tu hermanito, ¡no!

TELEHISTORIA ESCENA 1

Susana: Gracias, Papi, pero... ¿por qué no compras un carro nuevo? ¿un carro azul?

Classmate: Eh, Susanita, ¡qué divertido viajar en taxi todos los días...!

Salesclerk: ¿Quiere usted ver algo en especial?

Susana: A ver... ¿este anillo de oro?

Salesclerk: Claro que sí.

Susana: ¿Cuánto cuesta?

Salesclerk: Veinte mil colones.

Susana: ¡Uh! ¡Qué caro! Tengo diez mil colones, nada más.

Salesclerk: Señorita, no estamos en el mercado. Aquí no regateamos.

TELEHISTORIA ESCENA 2

Susana: Hmmm... ¡A mí me gustan mucho los collares de madera! ¡Uf! ¡Qué caro!

Salesclerk: ¡Buenos días! ¿Les puedo ayudar?

Susana: ¿Me deja ver esa joya? ¿Cuánto cuesta?

Salesclerk: Cuesta cincuenta mil colones. ¿Es un poco cara, verdad?

Jorge: A ti te gustan todas las cosas caras.

Salesclerk: ¿A usted le gustan los aretes de plata?

Jorge: Susana...

Susana: Y ahora, ¿qué te pasa a ti?

Video Scripts

TELEHISTORIA ESCENA 3

Salesclerk: ¿Y a usted no le gustan aquellos aretes de oro? ¿Ese collar de plata? ¿Estos anillos?

Jorge: Susana... ¡Allí está Trini Salgado, la jugadora de fútbol! Es ella, ¿no? ¿Qué está haciendo?

Susana: Sí, sí es ella. Está comprando unos aretes.

Jorge: ¡Vamos! Necesito su autógrafo, para Alicia. ¿Dónde está la camiseta de Alicia?

Susana: No sé.

COMPARACIÓN CULTURAL VIDEO

A typical vacation in Latin America takes you to craft markets and historical sites. But ecotourism is another type of tourism growing in popularity, especially in countries rich in natural beauty such as Costa Rica.

Costa Rica

Costa Rica has one of the most diverse ecosystems in the world. Here ecotourism has become very popular. It is a great way to learn first hand about different plants and animals that live in Costa Rica's protected areas.

There are many different types of eco-tours you can take in Costa Rica. There are over 51 types of birds and 583 different native plants found in the country, and if you are lucky you can also see deer, frogs, butterflies and monkeys.

Taking an eco-friendly vacation can provide you with rich and varied experiences. You can go hiking, sailing and snorkeling or bungee jumping.

Ecuador

Ecuador is another country with a very rich and biologically diverse environment. With terrain that goes from the mountain tops of the Andes down into the jungles of the Amazon, Ecuador is home to the rarely seen jaguar and other animals.

Puerto Rico

In Puerto Rico you can hike at El Yunque, the only Rain Forest in the US. The highest mountain rises 3523 feet above sea level. It gets 240 inches of rain a year! Perfect for tropical flowers, fern trees and the coqui, a tiny frog that lives in El Yunque.

If you ever have the chance to help plan a vacation, think of making a nature experience part of it. Costa Rica, Ecuador and Puerto Rico can provide an excellent opportunity for you to see some of the most unique and beautiful sceneries found in the world.

Audio Scripts

UNIDAD 8, LECCIÓN 1
TEXTBOOK SCRIPTS
TXT CD 8

PRESENTACIÓN DE VOCABULARIO

Level 1 Textbook pp. 410-411
Level 1B Textbook pp. 228-230
TXT CD 8, Track 1

A: ¡Hola! Me llamo Susana. En los días de escuela me acuesto muy temprano. Normalmente tengo que despertarme a las seis. Antes del desayuno voy al baño para lavarme la cara y maquillarme.

B: Generalmente mi hermano Jorge se levanta tarde y pasa mucho tiempo en el baño. Se afeita, se ducha y usa el secador de pelo para secarse el pelo. Siempre usa mi pasta de dientes para cepillarse los dientes. No es fácil vivir con él.

C: Después de peinarse y vestirse, Jorge se pone una chaqueta para ir a la escuela. Está contento porque mañana vamos de vacaciones.

D: Para las vacaciones, mi familia y yo vamos a hacer un viaje. A mí me gustaría ir a la ciudad, pero Jorge quiere ir al campo.

E: Mamá prefiere hacer un viaje en tren y papá quiere hacer un viaje en barco.

¡A RESPONDER!

Level 1 Textbook p. 411
TXT CD 8, Track 2
Level 1B Textbook p. 230
Level 1B TXT CD 2, Track 11

Escucha la rutina de Jorge. Mientras escuchas, representa las acciones.

1. Voy a despertarme temprano.
2. Voy a levantarme.
3. Voy a lavarme la cara.
4. Voy a afeitarme la cara.
5. Voy a lavarme el pelo.
6. Voy a peinarme.
7. Voy a cepillarme los dientes.
8. Voy a ponerme los zapatos.

TELEHISTORIA ESCENA 1

Level 1 Textbook p. 413
Level 1B Textbook p. 232
TXT CD 8, Track 3

Susana: Voy a hacer un viaje con mi familia. Podemos ir en avión, en barco...

Jorge: ¡Susana!

Susana: ¿Voy al campo o a la ciudad? El año pasado mi familia y yo fuimos al campo. Pero yo generalmente prefiero...

Jorge: ¡Susana! ¿Qué haces?

Jorge: Susana, ¿dónde está la leche?

Susana: ¡Mamá, papá!

Mamá: Susana, ¿qué?

Susana: Mi hermano es imposible. ¡Me voy a quedar en un hotel!

TELEHISTORIA ESCENA 2

Level 1 Textbook p. 418
Level 1B Textbook p. 238
TXT CD 8, Track 4

Susana: ¿Y mamá? ¿Dónde está?

Papá: En la oficina. Ahora ustedes tienen vacaciones, ¿no? ¿Qué planes tienen?

Jorge: Queremos ir a la playa el sábado. ¿Podemos?

Papá: Sí, pero el primer autobús a Playa Jacó sale a las nueve. Con tu rutina, Jorge, debes acostarte a las diez, para levantarte a las seis de la mañana. Necesitas tiempo para ducharte, lavarte el pelo, secarte el pelo, peinarte, ponerte la ropa...

Jorge: ¿Despertarme a las seis? Normalmente me levanto temprano y me visto rápidamente para ir a la escuela, pero ¡estoy de vacaciones! Papá, ¿podemos ir a la playa en carro?

Papá: No, tengo que ir a la oficina el sábado.

Jorge: ¿Puedo usar yo el carro?

ACTIVIDAD 10 (12) - LA RUTINA DE SUSANA

Level 1 Textbook p. 419
TXT CD 8, Track 5

Level 1B Textbook Act. 12 p. 239
Level 1B TXT CD 2, Track 12

Susana habla de lo que hace los sábados. Escucha la descripción y pon las fotos en orden según lo que dice. Luego escribe un párrafo para describir su rutina.

Hola, soy Susana. Me gustan los sábados porque no tengo que ir a la escuela. Generalmente me despierto tarde, a las once. Me gusta ducharme, pero los sábados normalmente me baño. Después me seco la cara. Luego me cepillo los dientes. Por fin me maquillo y salgo con los amigos. Los sábados me acuesto muy tarde, a las doce de la noche.

PRONUNCIACIÓN

Level 1 Textbook p. 419
Level 1B Textbook p. 239
TXT CD 8, Track 6

Los diptongos

In Spanish, vowels are divided into two categories: strong and weak. **A**, **e**, and **o** are the strong vowels; **i** and **u** are weak. A weak vowel with another vowel forms one sound, called a diphthong.

igualmente

demasiado

afeitarse

ciudad

If there are two consecutive vowels, and one has an accent mark, then each vowel is pronounced separately. The same is true for two strong vowels.

día

país

frío

leí

toalla

zoológico

peor

leer

Audio Scripts

TELEHISTORIA COMPLETA

Level 1 Textbook p. 423
Level 1B Textbook p. 244
TXT CD 8, Track 7

Escena 1 - Resumen

Susana va a hacer un viaje con su familia, pero su hermano, Jorge, es imposible.

Escena 2 - Resumen

Jorge y Susana quieren ir a la playa en coche el sábado, pero su padre tiene que ir a la oficina.

Escena 3

Susana: Jorge, estás comiendo y comiendo. ¡Por favor! ¿Quieres ir al centro comercial o no? Papá nos está esperando. Tiene que ir a la oficina.

Jorge, ¿no me escuchas? ¡Nos está llamando papá!

Jorge: Pero estoy comiendo el desayuno…

Susana: ¡Vamos, ahora! ¿No me estás escuchando? Papá está esperando. ¡Toma la mochila!

Jorge: Un momento, hay algo… Necesito algo importante. Pero, ¿qué puede ser?

ACTIVIDAD 18 (20) - INTEGRACIÓN

Level 1 Textbook p. 425
TXT CD 8, Track 8
Level 1B Textbook p. 246
Level 1B TXT CD 2, Track 13

Quieres hablar por Internet antes de las clases con dos amigos de Costa Rica. Lee el correo electrónico y escucha el mensaje telefónico. Decide si pueden hacerlo y explica por qué.

FUENTE 2 MENSAJE TELEFÓNICO

TXT CD 8, Track 9
Level 1B TXT CD 2, Track 14

Listen and take notes.

¿A qué hora se levantó hoy Carmen?

¿Cuándo está ocupada?

¿Cuándo puede estar en línea?

¡Hola! Soy yo, Carmen. Vamos a estar en línea mañana, ¿no?

Bueno… hoy, como siempre, me levanté a las seis menos diez. Me duché por veinte minutos y después de vestirme, preparé el almuerzo. Ahora me estoy cepillando el pelo y también me estoy maquillando un poco. Ya son las siete menos veinte. A las siete menos cuarto voy a caminar cuarenta y cinco minutos con mi perro. Tengo que salir a las ocho menos cuarto, y mis clases empiezan a las ocho. ¿Y tú? ¿Cuándo puedes estar en línea?

LECTURA: MI VIAJE A COSTA RICA

Level 1 Textbook pp. 426-427
Level 1B Textbook pp. 248-249
TXT CD 8, Track 10

El año pasado Sara y su familia hicieron un viaje a Costa Rica. Cuando volvieron a Miami, Sara hizo un álbum con fotos y recuerdos de sus experiencias.

Fuimos todos al bosque nuboso en Monteverde. Es una reserva biológica con muchos tipos de árboles y pájaros. Es un lugar ideal para caminar y tomar fotos. ¿Qué están mirando mi mamá y mis hermanos? No es un pájaro y no es un avión ... Es Papá.

¡Papá nunca tiene miedo! Aquí está en un zip line. Aquí va de árbol en árbol en un cable de metal.

Vimos un tucán. Es un pájaro bonito de muchos colores. Es típico de Costa Rica. Allí hay más de 850 especies de pájaros.

En San José, nos quedamos en un hotel en el centro. El hotel está cerca de la Plaza Central y la Catedral Metropolitana.

Un día fuimos a Escazú. Estoy comprando regalos para mis amigos en Miami. También compré una pequeña máscara de barro.

Hicimos un viaje en avión de San José a Tambor (en la costa del Pacífico de Costa Rica). Pasamos tres días en Montezuma. Descansamos en la playa, tomamos el sol y buceamos. ¡Fue mi parte favorita de las vacaciones!

REPASO DE LA LECCIÓN: ACTIVIDAD 1 – LISTEN AND UNDERSTAND

Level 1 Textbook p. 430
TXT CD 8, Track 11
Level 1B Textbook p. 252
Level 1B TXT CD 2, Track 15

Escucha a Silvia y a sus hermanos mientras se preparan para ir a la escuela. Indica lo que necesitan y explica por qué.

Silvia: Mamá…

Mamá: ¿Qué necesitas, Silvia?

Silvia: Estoy lavándome el pelo y necesito algo.

Roberto: Mamá…

Mamá: ¿Qué necesitas, Roberto?

Roberto: Me estoy secando la cara. Necesito algo.

Anita: Mamá…

Mamá: ¿Qué necesitas, Anita?

Anita: Voy a cepillarme los dientes pero necesito algo.

Juan: Mamá…

Mamá: ¿Qué, Juan?

Juan: No puedo secarme el pelo. Necesito algo.

Tomás: Mamá…

Mamá: ¿Qué, Tomás?

Tomás: Estoy lavándome la cara y necesito algo.

Laura: Mamá…

Mamá: ¿Qué necesitas, Laura?

Laura: Tengo que peinarme, pero necesito algo.

WORKBOOK SCRIPTS
WB CD 4

INTEGRACIÓN HABLAR

Level 1 Workbook p. 353
Level 1B Workbook p. 157
WB CD 4, Track 21

Listen to Agustín's message for his roommates. Take notes.

Copyright © by McDougal Littell, a division of Houghton Mifflin Company.

Audio Scripts

Audio Scripts

FUENTE 2

WB CD 4, Track 22

¡Hola a todos! Estoy pasando unas vacaciones divertidas. Llegué a un hotel muy bonito y, ¡qué divertido! Luego me bañé y me lavé el pelo, como todos los días. Tomé el sol y monté en bicicleta por el campo. Anoche, me acosté temprano y me dormí. El lugar es muy tranquilo. ¡El campo es lo mejor!

INTEGRACIÓN ESCRIBIR

Level 1 Workbook p. 354

Level 1B Workbook p. 158

WB CD 4, Track 23

Listen to Roberto's voicemail to Vilma. Take notes.

FUENTE 2

WB CD 4, Track 24

¡Hola, Vilma! Recibí tu correo electrónico. Yo lo estoy pasando muy bien en casa. Miro la televisión todo el día. Tengo muchas ideas para tus problemas. Puedes peinarte con el cepillo de dientes. También puedes lavarte el pelo con jabón. Y no tienes que salir a bailar. ¿Por qué no te acuestas temprano? ¡Ja, ja, ja, qué cómico! ¡No es cierto! Mañana, me despierto muy temprano y te mando todas las cosas que necesitas.

ESCUCHAR A, ACTIVIDAD 1

Level 1 Workbook p. 355

Level 1B Workbook p. 159

WB CD 4, Track 25

Listen to Fernando. Then, place an "x" next to the things that happened to him.

Hola, soy Fernando. No puedo despertarme temprano. Mi mamá me llama temprano y no puedo levantarme. Llego tarde a la escuela casi todos los días. De vez en cuando, si me acuesto temprano, puedo levantarme a las siete. Pero cuando me acuesto después de las ocho, no puedo. Mi mamá está enojada; dice que no puedo mirar la televisión por la noche.

ESCUCHAR A, ACTIVIDAD 2

Level 1 Workbook p. 355

Level 1B Workbook p. 159

WB CD 4, Track 26

Listen to Marta. Then, complete the sentences with the words from the box.

Hola, me llamo Marta y soy la mamá de Fernando. Mi hijo tiene un problema. Yo no sé qué podemos hacer. Se acuesta muy tarde y por la mañana no puede despertarse. Cuando se despierta, se baña, se afeita y se viste. Después va a la escuela pero casi siempre llega tarde. Cuando vuelve a casa, no quiere acostarse y otra vez está mirando la televisión o está escuchando música por la noche. Ya no sabemos qué hacer. Es su rutina.

ESCUCHAR B, ACTIVIDAD 1

Level 1 Workbook p. 356

Level 1B Workbook p. 160

WB CD 4, Track 27

Listen to Jorge. Then, complete the table with each person's routine.

Hola, me llamo Jorge. Mi rutina por la mañana es muy corta. Yo me despierto, me ducho, me cepillo los dientes y me lavo el pelo. Después me afeito y me visto. Yo lo hago en ¡veinte minutos! Pero mi hermana Daniela tiene una rutina muy diferente. Se despierta temprano, se lava el pelo, se cepilla los dientes y se baña. Después, se peina, se maquilla y se viste. Ella hace todo en ¡una hora y media!

ESCUCHAR B, ACTIVIDAD 2

Level 1 Workbook p. 356

Level 1B Workbook p. 160

WB CD 4, Track 28

Listen to Daniela. Then, complete the following sentences.

Buenos días, me llamo Daniela. En nuestra casa mi hermano y yo compartimos un baño. Es un problema porque yo necesito llegar a la escuela temprano todas las mañanas. Yo le digo a mi hermano que tiene que despertarse más temprano. Es una buena idea, pero a él no le gusta despertarse temprano. Él dice que no tengo que maquillarme en el espejo de baño pero no hay un espejo en mi cuarto.

ESCUCHAR C, ACTIVIDAD 1

Level 1 Workbook p. 357

Level 1B Workbook p. 161

WB CD 4, Track 29

Listen to Gabriela and take notes. Then, put her routine below in order, numbering the sentences 1 through 8.

Hola, me llamo Gabriela. Ésta es mi rutina de todas las mañanas. Primero, me despierto muy temprano y me lavo el pelo. Me cepillo los dientes después de bañarme. Me baño y me seco con la toalla. Después me seco el pelo con el secador de pelo. Busco mi ropa pero me maquillo antes de vestirme. Me maquillo en media hora. Antes de maquillarme me peino. En dos horas puedo salir del baño.

ESCUCHAR C, ACTIVIDAD 2

Level 1 Workbook p. 357

Level 1B Workbook p. 161

WB CD 4, Track 30

Listen to Gabriela's conversation with her mother. Take notes. Then, answer the following questions.

Mamá: ¡Gabriela! ¡Tu desayuno está en la mesa! ¿Qué estas haciendo?

Gabriela: En quince minutos voy, mamá, estoy maquillándome.

Mamá: Pero hija, no puedes salir antes de desayunar. ¿Puedes venir ahora? Tu padre y yo estamos saliendo ya para la oficina. ¡Necesitas desayunar antes de ir a la escuela!

ASSESSMENT SCRIPTS
TEST CD 2

LESSON 1 TEST: ESCUCHAR ACTIVIDAD A

Modified Assessment Book p. 278

On-level Assessment Book p. 353

Audio Scripts

Pre-AP Assessment Book p. 278
TEST CD 2, Track 19

Listen to the following audio. Then complete Activity A.

Generalmente me despierto a las siete de la mañana. No me gusta levantarme temprano pero necesito llegar temprano a la escuela. No me baño en la mañana. Prefiero bañarme en la noche. Cuando me levanto, me lavo la cara con jabón. Entonces me visto para la escuela. Siempre me pongo jeans y una camiseta. Entonces, como el desayuno con mi familia, me cepillo los dientes y a las siete y media voy a la escuela.

LESSON 1 TEST: ESCUCHAR ACTIVIDAD B

Modified Assessment Book p. 278
On-level Assessment Book p. 353
Pre-AP Assessment Book p. 278
TEST CD 2, Track 20

Listen to the following audio. Then complete Activity B.

Madre: Carlos, ¡come el desayuno! ¿Qué estás haciendo?

Carlitos: Mamá, me estoy cepillando los dientes.

Madre: Muy bien, Carlitos. ¿Estás usando mucha pasta de dientes?

Carlitos: Sí, mamá.

Madre: Carlitos, ya es tarde. ¿Qué estás haciendo?

Carlitos: Mamá, me estoy lavando la cara.

Madre: ¿Estás usando jabón?

Carlitos: Sí, mamá.

Madre: Carlitos, ¡ven a la cocina!

Carlitos: Mamá, me estoy poniendo mi ropa.

Madre: Muy bien, Carlitos. Debes ponerte los pantalones azules.

Carlitos: Sí, mamá.

Madre: Carlos, ya estoy enojada. ¿Qué estás haciendo?

Carlitos: Estoy jugando un videojuego en la computadora.

Madre: ¡Ay, Carlitos!

HERITAGE LEARNERS SCRIPTS
HL CDs 2 & 4

INTEGRACIÓN HABLAR

Level 1 HL Workbook p. 355
Level 1B HL Workbook p. 159
HL CD 2, Track 25

Escucha el mensaje del señor Amescua para su esposa. Puedes tomar apuntes mientras escuchas y luego responde a las preguntas.

FUENTE 2

HL CD 2, Track 26

¡Hola! Tengo una sorpresa. El señor Valle me aprobó las vacaciones. ¡Vámonos para Costa Rica! Ya hablé con nuestra agente de viajes y me dijo que por $ 1,799 podemos pasar 5 días en la playa. Todo está incluido: hotel, comidas, transporte, billetes de avión… ¿No te parece barato? Los niños se van a divertir mucho. El hotel tiene muchas actividades para ellos. ¡Ah! y en el spa nos darán un buen masaje y una buena limpieza facial. ¡No te parece increíble! Nos vemos a la hora de cenar.

INTEGRACIÓN ESCRIBIR

Level 1 HL Workbook p. 356
Level 1B HL Workbook p. 160
HL CD 2, Track 27

Escucha el anuncio de radio de un salón spa. Puedes tomar apuntes mientras escuchas y luego realiza la actividad.

FUENTE 2

HL CD 2, Track 28

Salón Diana le ofrece todo lo necesario para un día de relajamiento. Nuestra promoción de apertura permanecerá vigente toda la semana. Apúrese, quedan pocas citas disponibles. Salón Diana, un nuevo concepto en salud y belleza. Paquete de promoción Venus: Facial y masaje punto de presión $70. Paquete Artemisa: Desayuno, facial, masaje y acceso a piscina $95. Paquete Atenea: Renovación total. Para los que buscan una nueva imagen. $290. Incluye corte de cabello y maquillaje para las damas.

¡Haga su reservación hoy mismo!

LESSON 1 TEST: ESCUCHAR ACTIVIDAD A

HL Assessment Book p. 284
HL CD 4, Track 19

Escucha el siguiente audio. Luego, completa la Actividad A.

Madre: ¡Enrique! ¡Enrique! ¿Estás durmiendo, hijo mío? Tienes que levantarte ya. Tienes que llegar a la escuela temprano hoy.

Enrique: ¡Ay! ¿Qué me estás pidiendo? Me duele mucho el estómago.

Madre: ¿Qué me dices? No te duele nada. Vas a levantarte ahora y ducharte. Y no se te olvide peinarte bien, porque con estos pelos que llevas...

Enrique: Bien, bien. ¿No ves? Me levanto, me levanto.

Madre: Y después de lavarte el pelo, sécalo muy bien con la secadora porque hoy hace mucho frío.

Enrique: Muy bien, mamá.

Madre: ¡Ah! Y después de secarte, tienes que vestirte rápidamente porque te están esperando tus amigos Alfredo y José.

Enrique: ¿Alfredo y José, aquí?

Madre: Sí. Están comiendo el desayuno ahora y están hablando con papá.

Enrique: ¿Y de qué están hablando?

Madre: Están describiendo sus vacaciones en San José.

Enrique: ¿Y qué están diciendo de sus vacaciones?

Madre: Pero, Enrique, no debes estar hablando tanto y haciendo tantas preguntas... debes estar duchándote y vistiéndote. ¡Ahora!

Enrique: Bueno...

Audio Scripts

LESSON 1 TEST: ESCUCHAR ACTIVIDAD B

HL Assessment Book p. 284

HL CD 4, Track 20

Escucha el siguiente audio. Luego, completa la Actividad B.

Ana: Patricia, ¿adónde vamos de vacaciones mañana?

Patricia: Vamos a visitar a los abuelos.

Ana: ¿Y vamos a quedarnos en un hotel?

Patricia: No, Ana, vamos a quedarnos en casa de los abuelos. Tienen una casa muy grande. Viven en el campo.

Ana: ¿Está muy lejos de aquí su casa?

Patricia: Sí, Ana, está muy lejos. Tenemos que hacer el viaje en avión.

Ana: ¿Por qué no vamos en tren?

Patricia: Porque si hacemos el viaje en tren no llegamos en dos días. Con el avión llegamos en pocas horas.

Ana: ¿Y qué podemos hacer en el avión?

Patricia: Muchas cosas. Me gusta pasar el tiempo leyendo o escuchando música.

Ana: ¿Me lees un libro a mí en el avión?

Patricia: ¡Claro que sí! Vamos a llevar unos libros y los pongo en la mochila. Pero ahora tenemos que acostarnos porque mañana sale el avión muy temprano.

Ana: ¿A qué hora tenemos que levantarnos?

Patricia: A las cinco y media de la mañana porque el avión sale a las nueve menos cuarto.

Ana: Buenas noches, Patricia.

Patricia: Buenas noches, Ana. Hasta mañana.

Audio Scripts

UNIDAD 8, LECCIÓN 2
TEXTBOOK SCRIPTS
TXT CD 8

PRESENTACIÓN DE VOCABULARIO

Level 1 Textbook pp. 434-435

Level 1B Textbook pp. 256-258

TXT CD 8, Track 12

A. Estoy comiendo al aire libre con mi amiga. Es divertido, pero yo quisiera hacer un viaje al campo o al mar.

B. Me gustaría hacer surfing, hacer surf de vela, acampar o montar a caballo.

C. Cuando estoy de vacaciones siempre compro recuerdos en el mercado. Allí puedes regatear y las cosas son más baratas.

D. Hay artesanías y joyas de buena calidad. Quiero comprar un anillo de oro pero cuesta demasiado. Hay unos aretes de plata menos caros.

¡A RESPONDER!

Level 1 Textbook p. 435

TXT CD 8, Track 13

Level 1B Textbook p. 258

Level 1B TXT CD 2, Track 16

Escucha la lista de actividades que Susana quisiera hacer durante las vacaciones. Señala la foto correcta para cada actividad que menciona.

1. Me gustaría dar una caminata.

2. Quisiera hacer surfing.

3. Quisiera acampar.

4. Me gustaría hacer surf de vela.

5. Me gustaría hacer una parrillada.

6. Quisiera comer al aire libre.

7. Me gustaría montar a caballo.

TELEHISTORIA ESCENA 1

Level 1 Textbook p. 437

Level 1B Textbook p. 260

TXT CD 8, Track 14

Susana: Gracias, Papi. Pero, ¿por qué no compras un carro nuevo? ¿Un carro azul?

Amiga: Eh, Susanita, ¡qué divertido viajar en taxi todos los días!

Vendedora: ¿Quiere usted ver algo en especial?

Susana: A ver… ¿este anillo de oro?

Vendedora: Claro que sí.

Susana: ¿Cuánto cuesta?

Vendedora: Veinte mil colones.

Susana: ¡Qué caro! Tengo diez mil colones, nada más.

Vendedora: Señorita, no estamos en el mercado. Aquí no regateamos.

TELEHISTORIA ESCENA 2

Level 1 Textbook p. 442

Level 1B Textbook p. 266

TXT CD 8, Track 15

Susana: ¡A mí me gustan los collares de madera! ¡Qué caro!

Vendedor: ¡Buenos días! ¿Los puedo ayudar?

Susana: ¿Me deja ver esa joya? ¿Cuánto cuesta?

Vendedor: Cuesta cincuenta mil colones. Es un poco cara, ¿verdad?

Jorge: A ti te gustan todas las cosas caras.

Vendedor: ¿A usted le gustan los aretes de plata?

Jorge: Susana…

Susana: Y ahora, ¿qué te pasa a ti?

PRONUNCIACIÓN

Level 1 Textbook p. 443

Level 1B Textbook p. 267

TXT CD 8, Track 16

Unir las palbras

Native speakers may seem to speak quickly when they link their words in breath groups. Instead of pronouncing each word separately, they run some words together. This is common in all languages.

Listen and repeat.

¿A qué hora empieza el almuerzo?

Quisiera el anillo de oro y el artículo de madera.

Ella no puede acampar porque está ocupada.

ACTIVIDAD 12 (15) – ¿QUÉ ESTÁN HACIENDO?

Level 1 Textbook p. 445

TXT CD 8, Track 17

Level 1B Textbook p. 269

Level 1B TXT CD 2, Track 17

Hay muchas personas en el mercado hoy. Mira el dibujo y escucha las oraciones sobre qué están haciendo. Indica si cada oración es cierta o falsa.

1. Estas chicas están comprando collares.

2. Aquella señora está buscando un libro.

3. Esos señores están comprando cerámica.

4. Estas chicas están mirando ropa.

5. Aquel chico está comiendo helado.

6. Esa señora está vendiendo fruta.

TELEHISTORIA COMPLETA

Level 1 Textbook p. 447

Level 1B Textbook p. 272

TXT CD 8, Track 18

Escena 1 - Resumen

Jorge y Susana llegan al centro comercial. Susana quiere comprar un anillo, pero es muy caro.

Escena 2 - Resumen

Susana está hablando con el vendedor en la tienda cuando Jorge ve a alguien.

Escena 3

Vendedor: ¿Y a usted no le gustan aquellos aretes de oro? ¿Ese collar de plata? ¿Estos anillos?

Jorge: Susana, ¡allí está Trini Salgado, la jugadora de fútbol! Es ella, ¿no? ¿Qué está haciendo?

Susana: Sí, sí, es ella. Está comprando unos aretes.

Jorge: ¡Vamos! Necesito su autógrafo para Alicia. ¿Dónde está la camiseta de Alicia?

Susana: No sé…

ACTIVIDAD 18 (23) – INTEGRACIÓN

Level 1 Textbook p. 449

TXT CD 8, Track 19

Level 1B Textbook p. 274

Level 1B TXT CD 2, Track 18

Lee la guía y escucha el anuncio. Luego di qué te gustaría hacer allí y qué les vas a comprar a tu familia y amigos.

FUENTE 2

TXT CD 8, Track 20

Level 1B TXT CD 2, Track 19

Listen and take notes

¿Qué actividades hay en la playa?

¿Qué puedes hacer si no te gusta el mar?

¿Necesitas descansar en un lugar tranquilo? ¿O prefieres ir de compras y practicar deportes? En Playa Tamarindo vas a encontrar todo esto... y mucho más. Esta ciudad pequeña, con sus playas bonitas, es perfecta para las personas a quienes les gusta el mar. Aquí puedes estar en la playa todo el día: nadar y tomar el sol, y luego hacer una parrillada y comer al aire libre. Las personas más atléticas pueden hacer surfing, bucear o hacer surf de vela. Pero Tamarindo es más que una playa en el mar. Muchas personas vienen aquí para acampar y montar a caballo. ¡Hay actividades para todos! Llama a tu agente de viajes y ¡compra los boletos de avión ahora! Nos vemos... en Playa Tamarindo.

LECTURA CULTURAL: MERCADOS EN COSTA RICA Y URUGUAY

Level 1 Textbook pp. 450-451

Level 1B Textbook pp. 276-277

TXT CD 8, Track 21

En Latinoamérica, muchas ciudades tienen mercados al aire libre, donde puedes ir de compras y encontrar artículos interesantes y de buena calidad.

Audio Scripts

Es muy común regatear en los puestos de estos mercados. Si quieres regatear, hay algunas recomendaciones. Cuando escuchas el primer precio, puedes contestar: «¡Es demasiado!» También es importante ir a varios puestos para encontrar el precio más barato.

El Mercado Central de San José, Costa Rica, se fundó en el año 1880. En los puestos, venden una variedad de cosas, como café, frutas, verduras, pescado, carne, flores y plantas medicinales. También puedes comprar recuerdos. Hay camisetas, joyas y artículos de madera y de cuero. Si tienes hambre, hay restaurantes pequeños que se llaman sodas.

El Mercado del Puerto está cerca del mar en Montevideo, la capital de Uruguay. Se inauguró en 1868. Allí hay artistas locales que venden sus artículos y puedes comprar artesanías en las tiendas. También puedes comer en los restaurantes, donde sirven carne y pescado. La parrillada, un plato con diferentes tipos de carne, es muy popular. Los sábados, muchas personas van a este mercado para almorzar y escuchar música.

REPASO DE LA LECCIÓN: ACTIVIDAD 1 – LISTEN AND UNDERSTAND

Level 1 Textbook p. 454

TXT CD 8, Track 22

Level 1B Textbook p. 280

Level 1B TXT CD 2, Track 20

Escucha la conversación entre César y una vendedora. Luego escoge la respuesta correcta.

César: Buenas tardes, señora. Busco un recuerdo para una buena amiga.

Vendedora: ¿A ella le gustan las artesanías?

César: No. Prefiere las joyas. ¿Me deja ver aquellos anillos?

Vendedora: Claro que sí... Este anillo de oro es mi favorito.

César: Es muy bonito. ¿Cuánto cuesta?

Vendedora: Cuesta veinte mil colones.

César: ¡Uy! Es demasiado caro.

Vendedora: ¿Le gusta ese anillo de plata? Es bonito.

César: No, gracias. Mi amiga prefiere las joyas de oro.

Vendedora: Tengo unos aretes de oro de buena calidad. Le dejo los aretes en quince mil.

César: Está bien. Los voy a comprar.

COMPARACIÓN CULTURAL: ¡DE VACACIONES!

Level 1 Textbook pp. 456-457

Level 1B Textbook pp. 282-283

TXT CD 8, Track 23

Uruguay: Ernesto.

Ernesto: ¡Hola! Me llamo Ernesto y vivo en Montevideo. Es febrero, y mis padres y yo estamos de vacaciones en Punta del Este. Generalmente nos quedamos con mi abuela. Su casa está muy cerca de Playa Mansa. Es una playa donde el mar es muy tranquilo. Es ideal para nadar o tomar el sol. Yo prefiero ir a Playa Brava porque tiene más olas y es perfecta para hacer surfing. En las tardes me gusta pasear por el Mercado de los Artesanos. Allí les compro recuerdos a mis amigos.

Ecuador: Isabel.

Isabel: ¿Qué tal? Me llamo Isabel y soy de Quito. Mi familia y yo estamos pasando unos días de vacaciones en Baños, una ciudad que está en un valle, al lado de un volcán. Nos estamos quedando en un hotel que está muy cerca de las cascadas y de las aguas termales. Aquí puedes hacer muchas actividades al aire libre: montar a caballo, dar caminatas por la ruta de las cascadas y montar en bicicleta. ¡Es un lugar fenomenal!

Costa Rica: Osvaldo.

Osvaldo: ¡Hola! Me llamo Osvaldo y soy de Costa Rica. Estoy pasando las vacaciones de julio en el Parque Nacional Manuel Antonio. El hotel está en un bosque tropical lluvioso pero también tiene una playa en la costa del océano Pacífico. Todas las mañanas, mis padres y yo nos levantamos muy temprano y salimos a dar caminatas en el parque. Allí hay plantas y animales muy exóticos. ¡Me gusta estar en la naturaleza!

REPASO INCLUSIVO: ACTIVIDAD 1 – LISTEN, UNDERSTAND, AND COMPARE

Level 1 Textbook p. 458

Level 1B Textbook p. 284

TXT CD 8, Track 24

Listen to the telephone conversation between Mrs. Daza and her husband. Then answer the following questions.

Sra. Daza: Hola, Alberto. Te llamo porque todavía estoy trabajando en la oficina. Voy a llegar tarde a casa.

Sr. Daza: ¡Pero son las siete! ¿Qué pasó?

Sra. Daza: Hmmm... nada. Hay algunos problemas con el artículo que estoy escribiendo. Bueno... y tú, ¿qué hiciste hoy?

Sr. Daza: Después de trabajar, fui al mercado para comprar verduras. Cuando llegué a casa, preparé la cena: pescado, arroz con verduras...

Sra. Daza: ¿Ya terminaste la cena? ¿Y qué estás haciendo ahora?

Sr. Daza: Estoy escuchando música. ¡Pero aquí en casa... no hay nadie!

Sra. Daza: ¿No hay nadie? ¿Luisa y David no están allí?

Sr. Daza: No... aquí en la mesa hay un mensaje de David. Dice que está en la biblioteca.

Sra. Daza: Ah, entonces está estudiando. Debe llegar a las siete y media.

Sr. Daza: Y Luisa... no sé. Aquí no hay ningún mensaje de ella.

Sra. Daza: ¡Ah! Es verdad. Ella me llamó por teléfono a las cinco. Está en el teatro y está comprando las entradas. Vamos a ir todos este sábado, ¿no?

Sr. Daza: ¡¿Cómo?! ¡Pero yo las compré ayer!

WORKBOOK SCRIPTS
WB CD 4

INTEGRACIÓN HABLAR

Level 1 Workbook p. 376

Level 1B Workbook p. 180

WB CD 4, Track 31

Listen to what the announcer says through the loudspeakers at the Feria de Artesanías. Take notes.

FUENTE 2

WB CD 4, Track 32

¡Buenas tardes a todos! En nuestra feria de artesanías, pueden comprar joyas muy bonitas: anillos, collares y aretes de oro y plata. Si quieren llevar algunos recuerdos a sus amigos, les podemos ofrecer muchos artículos. Todos nuestros artículos son de gran calidad. ¿Cuánto cuestan? Tenemos una sorpresa: hoy todo es más barato. Pero hay que venir muy temprano para encontrar todos los mejores artículos.

INTEGRACIÓN ESCRIBIR

Level 1 Workbook p. 377

Level 1B Workbook p. 181

WB CD 4, Track 33

Listen to Federico's voice message to Olga. Take notes.

FUENTE 2

WB CD 4, Track 34

¡Hola, Olga! Estos días de vacaciones son muy buenos, pero estamos un poco tristes porque tú no estás. ¡Qué lástima! Pero, ¡te llevamos recuerdos! Yo te llevo artesanías de madera y Joaquín te lleva un collar. Hoy, pasamos todo el día en la playa. Hicimos muchas actividades. Hicimos surfing y también nadamos.

ESCUCHAR A, ACTIVIDAD 1

Level 1 Workbook p. 378

Level 1B Workbook p. 182

WB CD 4, Track 35

Listen to Cecilia talking about her vacation. Then, read each sentence and answer **cierto** (true) or **falso** (false).

Me llamo Cecilia. Me gustan las actividades al aire libre, como montar a

Copyright © by McDougal Littell, a division of Houghton Mifflin Company.

Audio Scripts

caballo, dar caminatas, acampar y hacer surfing. A mis amigos también les gustan estas actividades. Todas las vacaciones vamos a acampar en el campo. Estas vacaciones vamos a la playa. Somos doce chicos y chicas y a todos nos gusta hacer estas cosas.

ESCUCHAR A, ACTIVIDAD 2

Level 1 Workbook p. 378

Level 1B Workbook p. 182

WB CD 4, Track 36

Listen to Inés. Then, complete the sentences using the correct word in parentheses.

Me llamo Inés. Me voy de vacaciones con mis amigos. Ellos son chicos muy divertidos y les gusta hacer cosas que me gustan a mí. Yo también tengo una pelota para jugar. En el mercado de artesanías voy a comprarle a mi madre unos aretes como recuerdo.

ESCUCHAR B, ACTIVIDAD 1

Level 1 Workbook p. 379

Level 1B Workbook p. 183

WB CD 4, Track 37

Listen to Victoria. Then, draw lines to match each person with what he or she bought at the handicrafts market.

Ayer, mis amigos y yo fuimos al mercado de artesanías. Compramos todas estas cosas. Verónica le compró estos aretes de plata a su mamá. Hugo compró un artículo de madera muy bonito. Les compró este regalo a sus padres porque a ellos les gustan las artesanías. Mauro le compró un anillo a su amiga. Yo les compré algunos recuerdos a mis amigos de la escuela. Sandra me compró este collar.

ESCUCHAR B, ACTIVIDAD 2

Level 1 Workbook p. 380

Level 1B Workbook p. 183

WB CD 4, Track 38

Listen to Ernesto. Then, complete the following sentences.

Mi amiga Victoria fue de vacaciones y me compró un recuerdo muy bonito. Es un artículo de cerámica, una artesanía. Dice que no fue cara porque regateó y la persona de la tienda la dejó muy barata. Ella compró muchas, pensó en esto y las vendió baratas. Ella nos compró estos recuerdos a todos los chicos de la clase.

ESCUCHAR C, ACTIVIDAD 1

Level 1 Workbook p. 380

Level 1B Workbook p. 184

WB CD 4, Track 39

Listen to the handicrafts seller and take notes. Then, complete the chart.

Hoy vendí muchas artesanías. Llegó un grupo de estudiantes que están acampando cerca de la playa. Unos chicos compraron artículos de madera. Unas chicas compraron estos aretes de plata muy bonitos. Otras chicas compraron anillos de plata. Muchos chicos compraron recuerdos de cerámica para llevarles a sus amigos. Una chica compró un collar de oro muy caro.

ESCUCHAR C, ACTIVIDAD 2

Level 1 Workbook p. 380

Level 1B Workbook p. 184

WB CD 4, Track 40

Listen to Miriam and take notes. Then, answer the questions with complete sentences.

Hoy le compré un collar de oro a mi mamá. A ella le gustan estas joyas. Le gusta mucho el oro y le gusta más si es una artesanía. Estos collares le gustan mucho. No le compré nada a mi papá porque compré este collar y ya no tengo más dinero. Este collar es muy caro.

ASSESSMENT SCRIPTS TEST CD 2

LESSON 2 TEST: ESCUCHAR ACTIVIDAD A

Modified Assessment Book p. 290

On-level Assessment Book p. 370

Pre-AP Assessment Book p. 290

TEST CD 2, Track 21

Listen to the following audio. Then complete Activity A.

¿Piensa usted ir de vacaciones? Ofrecemos dos viajes ideales.

Primero, una semana en la playa de Costa Rica. No hay nada mejor que nadar en el mar. Son cinco noches en un hotel muy bueno cerca de la playa con los mejores restaurantes. También hay clases de tres deportes acuáticos: surf, esquí acuático y surf de vela. Si prefiere, puede pasar el rato montando a caballo en la playa y mirando la naturaleza.

El segundo viaje es al campo. Venga con nosotros a acampar en las montañas de Costa Rica. Estas vacaciones le van a encantar. Usted va dormir al aire libre y dar caminatas por las montañas. Nosotros lo podemos llevar y traer y le damos todo lo que necesita para acampar. La comida es muy nutritiva. Hay verduras y carne para hacer parrilladas. Es un viaje ideal para unas vacaciones muy divertidas.

LESSON 2 TEST: ESCUCHAR ACTIVIDAD B

Modified Assessment Book p. 290

On-level Assessment Book p. 370

Pre-AP Assessment Book p. 290

TEST CD 2, Track 22

Listen to the following audio. Then complete Activity B.

Sara: Señora, ¿me deja ver esos aretes, por favor?

Señora: ¿Estos aretes de oro, o esos aretes de plata?

Sara: Los de plata, por favor.

Señora: Esos cuestan 30 dólares.

Sara: ¡Qué caro!

Señora: Son de muy buena calidad, pero los dejo en veinticinco.

Sara: Son muy bonitos pero no tengo mucho dinero. Le puedo ofrecer quince dólares.

Señora: No es posible. Pero le dejo aquel anillo de plata en quince dólares.

Sara: Pero quisiera los aretes también.

Señora: Bueno, le dejo los aretes y el anillo en 30 dólares.

Sara: Está bien. Muchas gracias.

UNIT 8 TEST: ESCUCHAR ACTIVIDAD A

Modified Assessment Book p. 302

On-level Assessment Book p. 382

Pre-AP Assessment Book p. 302

TEST CD 2, Track 23

Listen to the following audio. Then complete Activity A.

Ana: ¡Hola! Me llamo Ana. Normalmente me levanto a las siete de la mañana. Me baño y me lavo el pelo todos los días. Necesito una hora para bañarme y siempre me seco el pelo con el secador de pelo. Me maquillo todos los días. Después de bañarme y maquillarme me visto para ir a la escuela. Es muy importante vestirme bien para mi escuela.

Eva: ¡Hola! Me llamo Eva. Mi rutina en la mañana es un poco diferente que la rutina de mi hermana Ana. Yo necesito menos tiempo en la mañana que ella. Me gusta levantarme tarde, a las diez de la mañana. Siempre me baño pero yo necesito cinco minutos para bañarme. Si tengo tiempo, me lavo el pelo pero no me lavo el pelo todos los días. Tengo un secador de pelo pero nunca lo uso. Nunca me maquillo. No me gusta maquillarme. No necesito mucho tiempo para vestirme.

UNIT 8 TEST: ESCUCHAR ACTIVIDAD B

Modified Assessment Book p. 302

On-level Assessment Book p. 382

Pre-AP Assessment Book p. 302

TEST CD 2, Track 24

Listen to the following audio. Then complete Activity B.

Verónica: ¡Qué joyas tan bonitas!

Vendedora: Muchas gracias, señorita.

Audio Scripts

Verónica: Me gusta este anillo. ¿Me lo deja ver?

Vendedora: Claro que sí.

Verónica: ¿Cuánto cuesta?

Vendedora: Cuesta doscientos dólares.

Verónica: ¡Qué caro! Le puedo ofrecer cien dólares.

Vendedora: Lo siento, señorita. Aquí no regateamos.

Verónica: Lo siento, es demasiado caro. Buenos días. ¡Qué cosas tan bonitas tiene! ¿Me deja ver los aretes?

Vendedor: Claro que sí. Son de oro. Buena calidad.

Verónica: ¿Cuánto cuestan?

Vendedor: Cuestan setenta y cinco dólares pero para usted le dejo los aretes en sesenta dólares.

Verónica: Le puedo ofrecer cincuenta dólares pero es todo.

Vendedor: Bueno, señorita, cincuenta dólares. Aquí tiene sus aretes.

FINAL EXAM: ESCUCHAR
ACTIVIDAD A

Modified Assessment Book p. 314

On-level Assessment Book p. 394

Pre-AP Assessment Book p. 314

TEST CD 2, Track 25

Listen to the following audio. Then complete Activity A.

1. Hola, mi problema es que tengo que trabajar mucho en casa y no tengo tiempo para salir. Estoy muy cansado. Yo lavo los platos, limpio la cocina, plancho la ropa y paso la aspiradora.

2. Hola, yo juego con el equipo de fútbol de mi escuela. Nosotros corremos mucho todos los días. Es muy difícil. No puedo correr más.

3. No fui a la escuela hoy. Me quedé en casa. Me duele la cabeza y me duele el estómago. Necesito dormir.

4. ¿Qué hago? Tengo que hacer la tarea para mañana y no puedo usar mi computadora. No puedo escribir en el teclado. ¡No sé qué hacer!

5. Mis amigos fueron al cine pero no me invitaron. Estoy en casa y quiero salir. Estoy muy triste.

FINAL EXAM: ESCUCHAR
ACTIVIDAD B

Modified Assessment Book p. 314

On-level Assessment Book p. 394

Pre-AP Assessment Book p. 314

TEST CD 2, Track 26

Listen to the following audio. Then complete Activity B.

Hola, Laura. Pienso que no estás en casa. Yo pasé un fin de semana muy divertido.

Sábado por la tarde fui al parque de diversiones con mi hermano. Subimos a la montaña rusa. ¡Qué miedo! En la noche practiqué el básquetbol en el gimnasio con mis primos. ¿Y tú? ¿Estás bien? ¿Quieres acompañarme a la fiesta de mi abuela mañana? Damos una fiesta para celebrar su cumpleaños. Mañana, voy a levantarme a las ocho. Por favor llámame en mi casa. Está bien si quieres llamarme temprano o puedes mandarme un correo electrónico. Hasta luego.

HERITAGE LEARNERS SCRIPT
HL CDs 2 & 4

INTEGRACIÓN HABLAR

Level 1 HL Workbook p. 378

Level 1B HL Workbook p. 182

HL CD 2, Track 29

Escucha el mensaje que Ángeles Robles le dejó a su hija Fernanda. Toma notas mientras escuchas y prepárate para responder a las preguntas.

FUENTE 2

HL CD 2, Track 30

Aló, Fernanda. Nunca estás en casa, hija. Mira, te dejo la lista de las personas a quienes debes traerles un recuerdito sin falta. Aquí no hay excusas, hija. Te deposité dinero en la cuenta de banco o puedes usar tu tarjeta de crédito. Como tú prefieras pero no quiero que bajes del avión sin regalos para tu abuela Agustina, tu abuelo Rami, claro, tu tío Sergio y tu tía Chabela. No te olvides de regatear si vas de compras a un mercado. Por mí y tu papá no te preocupes. Aunque ya sabes cómo me gusta la joyería… Bueno, te hablo más tarde y nos vemos mañana. Ay, hija, te extraño mucho.

INTEGRACIÓN ESCRIBIR

Level 1 HL Workbook p. 379

Level 1B HL Workbook p. 183

HL CD 2, Track 31

Escucha el mensaje que le dejó a su familia Gonzalo Alarcón, un estudiante estadounidense que hace un intercambio en Costa Rica. Puedes tomar notas mientras escuchas y luego completa la actividad.

FUENTE 2

HL CD 2, Track 32

Papá, necesito que me digas qué comprarle a cada persona en la familia. Ya sabes que soy malísimo para esto. Así que si me recomiendas qué y dónde comprar los recuerdos de mamá, mi hermana Lorena, el tuyo y el de mis primos Pedro y Juan, te lo voy a agradecer siempre. Gracias por el dinero que me mandaste. Ya me hacía falta. Bueno, hasta pronto, Gonzalo.

LESSON 2 TEST: ESCUCHAR
ACTIVIDAD A

HL Assessment Book p. 296

HL CD 4, Track 21

Escucha el siguiente audio. Luego, completa la actividad A.

¡Hola! Soy José y estoy de vacaciones en el campo con mi familia. ¡Y no me gusta nada! Prefiero la ciudad. En la ciudad puedo hacer muchísimas cosas. Puedo ir al cine y al teatro, visitar los museos e ir al centro comercial con mis amigos. Aquí, en el campo no hay centros comerciales ni restaurantes. En el campo no puedo ir a conciertos. Por eso vengo con muchos discos compactos para escuchar la música que a mí me gusta... y no la música que les gusta escuchar a mis padres. Sé que a mis padres y hermanos les gusta dar caminatas muy largas por el campo. Dicen que es muy sano. Yo prefiero pasar el tiempo libre mirando la televisión, pero en el campo no hay televisión. Estamos cerca de la playa y todos hacen surf de vela y surfing. Todos menos yo. ¡No sé nadar! Y mañana tenemos que levantarnos a las seis de la mañana. ¡A las seis y estamos de vacaciones! Vamos a montar a caballo. Es idea de mi hermana mayor porque a ella le gustan los caballos y el campo. ¡Ay de mí, no estoy nada contento!

LESSON 2 TEST: ESCUCHAR
ACTIVIDAD B

HL Assessment Book p. 296

HL CD 4, Track 22

Escucha el siguiente audio. Luego, completa la actividad B.

Vendedor: Buenas tardes, señorita.

Beatriz: Buenas tardes. Quisiera ver unos aretes, por favor.

Vendedor: ¿De oro o de plata?

Beatriz: ¿Cuánto cuestan los de oro?

Vendedor: Generalmente, cuestan 25,000 colones, pero hoy le puedo ofrecer estos aretes en 23,000 colones.

Beatriz: ¡Son demasiado caros!

Vendedor: ¿Cómo cuánto quiere gastar? Porque tenemos una gran selección de otros artículos de regalo: cerámicas, artículos típicos de Costa Rica como carretas, tucanes y quetzal es de madera...

Beatriz: ¿Cuánto cuesta ese quetzal?

Vendedor: ¿Ese de madera o aquel quetzal de plata?

Beatriz: El quetzal de madera, porque pienso que el de plata cuesta mucho, ¿no?

Vendedor: Pues, mire: el quetzal de madera cuesta 30,000 colones porque es de artesanía y el artista es muy famoso. El quetzal de plata es pequeñito y el precio es 10,000 colones.

Beatriz: ¿Me deja ver las cerámicas, por favor?

Vendedor: Sí, sí, son de muy buena calidad y son típicas de San José. Éstas

Audio Scripts

grandes cuestan 12,000 colones y las pequeñas, tan sólo 8,000.

Beatriz: Me gustan las pequeñas. Son dos recuerdos para mis dos abuelas. Y me gustaría darle a mi madre el quetzal de plata. ¿Le puedo ofrecer 15,000 por todo?

Vendedor: Quince mil colones son poco. Le puedo ofrecer todo por 16,500.

Beatriz: Está bien.

UNIT 8 TEST: ESCUCHAR ACTIVIDAD A

HL Assessment Book p. 308

HL CD 4, Track 23

Escucha el siguiente audio. Luego, completa la actividad A.

Vendedora: Buenas tardes. Son muy bonitos estos collares, ¿no?

Cliente: Sí, sí, son bonitos. ¿Cual es el precio?

Vendedora: Los de oro cuestan 45,000 colones y los de plata, 25,000.

Cliente: ¡Qué caros son!

Vendedora: Son de artesanía, y de oro o de plata.

Cliente: Pero soy estudiante. No tengo mucho dinero.

Vendedora: ¿Cuánto quieres gastar?

Cliente: Bueno... quiero comprarles recuerdos a mis amigos en los Estados Unidos.

Vendedora: ¿Qué tal te parecen esos artículos de madera? Son muy típicos del país. Uno es un tucán y otro es un quetzal.

Cliente: ¿Me deja verlos?

Vendedora: Claro que sí. Son muy bonitos, ¿no?

Cliente: Sí, son bonitos y son pequeños. Los puedo poner en la mochila. ¿Cuánto cuestan?

Vendedora: Mira, normalmente cuestan 8,000 colones, pero si compras dos, te puedo ofrecer dos por 14,000. ¿Bien?

Cliente: Y si compro cuatro, ¿cuánto es?

Vendedora: Te dejo los cuatro por 26,000 colones.

Cliente: ¿Y no puede dejarme los cuatro por 24,000?

Vendedora: Por 24,000, no. Pero por 25,000...

Cliente: ¡Muy bien! ¿Y cuánto cuestan las carretas?

Vendedora: Cuestan 5,000 colones.

Cliente: ¿Y si compro cuatro?

Vendedora: Dieciocho mil.

Cliente: ¿Y no me puede bajar el precio si... si compro esos aretes de plata?

Vendedora: Bueno, si compras estos aretes por 20,000, te puedo ofrecer las cuatro carretas por 15,000 colones.

Cliente: Perfecto. ¿Me los puede envolver, por favor?

UNIT 8 TEST: ESCUCHAR ACTIVIDAD B

HL Assessment Book p. 308

HL CD 4, Track 24

Escucha el siguiente audio. Luego, completa la actividad B.

¡Ufff! Hay tantas cosas que tengo que hacer antes de ir a la escuela. Ya hice una de ellas: me desperté. Ahora me estoy levantando... vamos a ver: ¿tengo que esperar para entrar al baño? ¡No! Estoy en la ducha, pero el agua está muy fría. Brrr.... Mis hermanos se ducharon antes y ya no queda agua caliente. Bueno, me ducho en un minuto. A ver, ¿dónde está el jabón? ¡Es tan pequeño! Mis hermanos usaron casi todo el jabón y tampoco queda mucho champú. Bueno, una ducha de menos de un minuto. Ahora me seco... ¿pero dónde están las toallas grandes? ¡Tengo frío! Claro, mis hermanos llevaron todas las toallas a su cuarto y las dejaron en el suelo. Bueno, me seco con esta toallita pequeña. Y ahora, a cepillarme los dientes. Aquí está mi cepillo, la pasta de dientes... ¡Pero si no hay pasta para limpiar ni un diente! ¡Ay, mis hermanos la usaron y no compraron más! Bueno, pero aquí está el peine y el secador de pelo... Ahora me visto. ¿Pero dónde están los jeans nuevos? ¿Y la camiseta que compré ayer? ¿Por qué siempre me causan tantos problemas mis hermanos?

FINAL EXAM: ESCUCHAR ACTIVIDAD A

HL Assessment Book p. 320

HL CD 4, Track 25

Escucha el siguiente audio. Luego, completa la actividad A.

La señora: ¿Aló?

Ricardo: Buenos días, señora, soy Ricardo. ¿Está Amelia, por favor?

La señora: Sí, está. Un momentito.

Amelia: ¡Hola, Ricardo! ¡Qué tal las vacaciones?

Ricardo: Muy bien, Amelia. Las pasamos fenomenal.

Amelia: ¿Cuando volvieron ustedes?

Ricardo: Anoche. Llegamos a las once, por eso no te llamé porque a esas horas estás durmiendo.

Amelia: Sí, generalmente me acuesto a las diez. Pero dime: ¿qué hiciste?

Ricardo: Pues, hice muchas cosas. El primer día, fuimos a la playa e hice surfing. Fue muy divertido. El segundo día montamos a caballo.

Amelia: ¿Y adónde fueron a caballo?

Ricardo: Subimos por las montañas, vimos un volcán y luego bajamos a la playa.

Amelia: ¿Y dónde se quedaron? ¿Acamparon?

Ricardo: ¡No, no! No acampamos. Nos gusta hacer actividades al aire libre, pero preferimos estar en un hotel.

Amelia: ¿Y qué te pareció la comida? ¿Te gustó?

Ricardo: Mucho. Comí unos platos típicos como el gallo pinto, la sopa negra y el casado.

Amelia: ¿Y visitaste algún mercado?

Ricardo: Bueno, yo no visité ninguno porque no me gusta ir de compras, pero mis padres fueron a un mercado muy interesante con mi hermana, Regatearon mucho y compraron muchos recuerdos. Hay algo especial para ti.

Amelia: ¡Muchas gracias!

Ricardo: De nada, Amelia. Me gustaría verte hoy para darte el recuerdo.

Amelia: Muy bien, pero acabo de despertarme. Tengo que ducharme y comer algo. ¿Por qué no vienes a las once?

Ricardo: Muy bien. Te veo a las once.

FINAL EXAM: ESCUCHAR ACTIVIDAD B

HL Assessment Book p. 320

HL CD 4, Track 26

Escucha el siguiente audio. Luego, completa la actividad B.

Laura, soy Pili. Te puedo acompañar a la feria por la tarde porque acabo de terminar todos los quehaceres. Primero hice todas las camas; luego lavé los platos del desayuno, limpié la cocina y saqué la basura. Ahora estoy escuchando el nuevo disco compacto que compré anoche. ¿A qué hora quieres salir? Llámame.

Laura, soy Bárbara y acabo de buscar tus apuntes por toda la casa, pero no los encuentro. ¿Por qué no llamas a Pedro? A veces él pone tus cosas en su mochila. Esta mañana estoy decorando la casa porque por la noche vamos a celebrar el cumpleaños de mi madre. Viene toda la familia... pero es un secreto. ¡Qué divertido va a ser! ¿Quieres pasar por aquí y tomar un poco de pastel y cantar "Cumpleaños feliz"? Si quieres, ven alrededor de las nueve... ¿vale?

Oye, Laura, soy Federico. ¿Qué quieres hacer esta noche? ¿Quieres acompañarme al parque de diversiones? Tengo cuatro boletos. ¿Invitamos a Antonio y Ana también? Ayer le ayudé a mi primo David. Él acaba de comprar un apartamento y le ayudé a subir muebles. Me duelen mucho las piernas y los brazos, pero ahora estoy descansando y pienso que esta noche voy a estar mejor. Llámame.

Map/Culture Activities Costa Rica

1 Costa Rica is a Central American country known for its extensive coastline and beautiful beaches. Which body of water lies to the northeast of Costa Rica? Which lies to the southwest? Label each body of water on the map.

2 **Cordilleras**, or mountain ranges, run down the center of Costa Rica from northwest to southeast. They surround the **Meseta Central**, or Central Plateau, where about 75 percent of Costa Rica's population lives and where its capital city is located. Find this city and write its name on the map.

3 Puntarenas is home to Costa Rica's most important fishing port and therefore is known for being a great place to get excellent seafood. Locate this town and write its name on the map.

4 In 1502, Christopher Columbus landed near what is now the city of Limón. Find this port town and write its name on the map.

5 About three-fourths of Costa Rica's southernmost peninsula on its Pacific side has been declared a national park or forest reserve. Locate this peninsula and label it on the map.

UNIDAD 8 Map/Culture Activities

Map/Culture Activities *Costa Rica*

6 Is each sentence below true or false? Use the information from the cultural pages in your book to decide. Circle **C** for **cierto** and **F** for **falso**. If a sentence is false, circle the word or phrase that is incorrect and write the correct one below.

1. El dinero de Costa Rica fue nombrado por (*was named for*) un explorador muy famoso.   C   F

_____

2. Las carretas de Costa Rica fueron usadas para transportar bananas.   C   F

_____

3. Costa Rica está en América Central, entre Panamá y El Salvador.   C   F

_____

4. Según los costarriqueños, las aguas termales de Tabacón son buenas para la salud.   C   F

_____

7 Costa Rica has a tropical climate characterized by warm weather and substantial yearly rainfall. What is the climate like where you live? How is it similar or different?

_____

_____

_____

_____

8 Costa Rica's extensive coastline and tropical climate make it the perfect place to enjoy water sports such as surfing, kayaking, and water skiing. Are these sports popular where you live? Why or why not?

_____

_____

_____

_____

UNIDAD 8

Map/Culture Activities

Map/Culture Activities Answer Key

COSTA RICA
Page 83

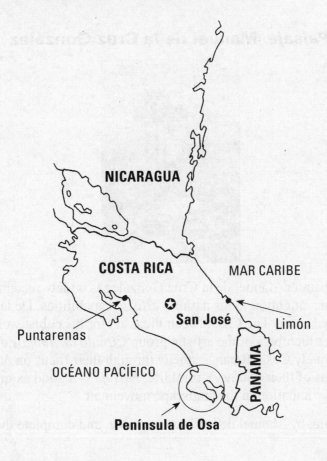

NICARAGUA

COSTA RICA

MAR CARIBE

San José

Limón

Puntarenas

OCÉANO PACÍFICO

PANAMA

Península de Osa

1. See map above. (Mar Caribe, Océano Pacífico)
2. See map above.
3. See map above.
4. See map above.
5. See map above.
6.
   1. C
   2. F <u>bananas</u>: café
   3. F <u>El Salvador</u>: Nicaragua
   4. C
7. Answers will vary.
8. Answers will vary.

Fine Art Activities

Paisaje, Manuel de la Cruz González

Costa Rican writer and painter Manuel de la Cruz González is widely recognized for helping bring international attention to his nation's artistic capabilities. De la Cruz González often is referred to as "The Costa Rican Picasso" for his cubist works; however, he and the other members of the artistic group *Círculo de Amigos del Arte* helped create a uniquely Costa Rican aesthetic through their focus on native landscapes and depictions of their country's rural life. *Paisaje* is a good example of de la Cruz González's participation in the landscape movement.

Study the painting *Paisaje*, by Manuel de la Cruz González, and complete the following activities.

1. Would you describe the colors as bright or subdued? Why?

_____

_____

_____

_____

2. Observe the way in which the natural landscape interacts with the houses. Tell whether you think the two elements of the painting work together or against one another and explain why.

_____

_____

_____

_____

_____

Paisaje (undated), Manuel de la Cruz González. Tempera on wood, 33 cm x 29 cm. Courtesy of Galería 11-12, San José, Costa Rica.

Fine Art Activities

Surcando aires, Adrián Gómez

Children on swings are a favorite subject of Costa Rican artist Adrián Gómez. Gómez is known for his use of soft colors and open space to create a sense of lightness and movement. The ability to capture the essence of children in motion is reflected in the work *Surcando aires*.

Study *Surcando aires* by Adrián Gómez and complete the following activities.

1. Do you think the medium and colors chosen in *Surcando aires* are appropriate for the subject? If you do, explain why. If you don't, tell what medium and colors you would have used instead.

   _____

   _____

   _____

   _____

   _____

2. *Surcando aires* depicts a child on a swing against a wash of blue and yellow. Why do you think Gómez chose to exclude a figurative background? Discuss the effect this decision has on the work.

   _____

   _____

   _____

   _____

   _____

   _____

Surcando aires (2002), Adrián Gómez. Acrílico sobre tela, 55 cm x 75 cm. Courtesy of the artist.

Fine Art Activities

Midiendo café, Antonio Mejía

Antonio Mejía is a contemporary Costa Rican artist whose expressive paintings focus on everyday life. His choice of subject and use of bright colors give his work a strong sense of activity and movement. Many of his paintings, like *Midiendo café*, show the interconnectedness between the Costa Rican people and their environment.

Complete the following activities based on your interpretations of *Midiendo café* by Antonio Mejía.

1. Scan the painting and mark an **X** next to those things you see in the painting.

☐ A woman holding a baby   ☐ A child sorting coffee beans

☐ People picking coffee beans   ☐ Three men arguing

☐ A bird in a tree   ☐ A woman wearing an orange skirt

☐ A man pointing   ☐ A man loading coffee beans onto a cart

☐ A rainbow in the distance   ☐ A snake in a bush

2. Tell which aspects of *Midiendo café* first called your attention and explain why.

_____

_____

_____

3. How does Mejía capture a sense of motion in *Midiendo café*? Describe the ways in which the artist uses posture to suggest movement in the painting.

_____

_____

_____

_____

Midiendo café (2004), Antonio Mejía. Oil on canvas, 56 cm x 75 cm. Courtesy of Galería Valanti, San José, Costa Rica.

Fine Art Activities

Familia en el volcán Arenal, Jeannette Carballo

The term *folk art* is used to describe the work of individuals with little or no formal artistic training. Although folk art often reflects a lack of technical mastery, its characteristic bright colors, decorative appeal, and emphasis on cultural realism ensure its place in the art world. Many folk artists, like Costa Rican painter Jeannette Carballo, focus on the everyday activities and practices of their local communities.

Study *Familia en el volcán Arenal* by Jeannette Carballo and complete the following activities.

1. Observe the volcano in the background. Do you think the artist meant to portray the volcano as majestic or as ominous?

   _____

   _____

   _____

2. Review the brief explanation of folk art in the introduction. Explain how *Familia en el volcán Arenal* identifies or doesn't identify Carballo as a folk artist and support your opinion with specific examples from the painting.

   _____

   _____

   _____

   _____

   _____

   _____

Familia en el volcán Arenal (1989), Jeannette Carballo. Oil on canvas. 100 cm x 72 cm. Courtesy of the artist.

Fine Art Activities Answer Key

PAISAJE, MANUEL DE LA CRUZ GONZÁLEZ, p. 86

1a. Answers will vary. Suggestion: Although the artist uses red, green, yellow, and white in the painting, the tones are muted. The subdued shades used suggest a hazy or overcast day, reinforced by the appearance of gray rain clouds.

b. Answers will vary. Suggestion: The artist achieves color balance in the painting by including the same or similar shades of a color at the top, in the middle, and on the bottom of the painting. From top to bottom, the gray-blue of the clouds is repeated in the rooftops, the rocks by the lake, and in the lake itself. The green foliage of the tree extends almost to the top of the painting, bringing the color green upwards from the hills and grass.

2. Answers will vary. Suggestion: Both the natural landscape and the human landscape are painted in a similar palette of subdued tones, which makes the houses appear to blend into the landscape. The gray used in the sky and stones is also used on the rooftops, making them seem as if they might be part of the natural setting.

SURCANDO AIRES, ADRIÁN GÓMEZ, p. 87

1. Answers will vary. Students should be able to back up their opinion with specifics from the painting

2. Answers will vary. Students may suggest that the open background evokes a sense of freedom or of flying.

MIDIENDO CAFÉ, ANTONIO MEJÍA, p. 88

1a. Marked items should be: A woman holding a baby; People picking coffee beans; A man pointing; A child sorting coffee beans; A woman wearing an orange skirt; A man loading coffee beans onto a cart

2. Answers will vary. Suggestion: Students may focus on the landscape, the work of harvesting and measuring raw coffee beans, or the variety of people and animals shown in the painting.

3. Answers will vary. Suggestion: Although the painting is static, Mejía captures the animals and people in the painting in a state of activity. The postures of the subjects are fluid, natural, and immediately recognizable; the viewer can imagine the next seconds of the scene. The dog sniffing the ground, the woman rocking the baby, the coffee beans falling out of the basket into the cart, the oxen shifting their feet, the two men facing forward talking to the man in the blue shirt, etc.

FAMILIA EN EL VOLCÁN ARENAL, JEANNETTE CARBALLO, p. 89

1. Answers will vary. Students should be able to explain their reactions by calling on certain aspects of the painting.

2. Answers will vary. Students may focus on the bright colors used, the lack of sophistication of the human figures, or the depiction of a local family.

Date: _____

Dear Family:

We are about to begin *Unidad 8* of the Level 1 *¡Avancemos!* program. It focuses on authentic culture and real-life communication using Spanish in Costa Rica. It practices reading, writing, listening, and speaking, and introduces students to culture typical of Costa Rica.

Through completing the activities, students will employ critical thinking skills as they compare the Spanish language and the culture of Costa Rica with their own community. They will also connect to other academic subjects, using their knowledge of Spanish to access new information. In this unit, students are learning to talk about a typical day, what they are doing, their daily routine while on vacation, buying souvenirs on vacation, and vacation activities. They are also learning about grammar—reflexive verbs, present progressive, indirect object pronouns, and demonstrative adjectives.

Please feel free to call me with any questions or concerns you might have as your student practices reading, writing, listening, and speaking in Spanish.

Sincerely,

Family Involvement Activity

Broken Phone Line

STEP 1

Sit with your family members around a table or on a couch so that you form a line. The aim of the game is to see how far your message gets toward the end of the line without being changed.

STEP 2

The first person in line invents a message using the lesson vocabulary. This player whispers the message, clearly but quickly—and only one time—into the ear of the person sitting to his or her right.

STEP 3

The second player whispers what he or she heard into the next person's ear. Play until everyone has heard the message. The last to hear the message tells the group what he or she has heard.

STEP 4

The person who first distorted the message moves to the end of the line. Start again with a new message. The first person in line stays in that position until all players pass the message without any change. Then he or she goes to the end of the line. The second person in line then creates messages.

Each time a sentence reaches the last person in line without alteration, write the sentence below:

_____

_____

_____

_____

_____

Absent Student Copymasters

Presentación / Práctica de vocabulario

Materials Checklist

- [ ] Student text
- [ ] DVD 2
- [ ] Video activities copymasters
- [ ] TXT CD 8 tracks 1–2
- [ ] LIB TXT CD 2 track 11
- [ ] *Cuaderno* pages 344–346 (L1B pp. 148–150)
- [ ] *Cuaderno para hispanohablantes* pages 344–347 (L1B pp. 148–151)
- [ ] Did You Get It? Copymasters 1, 2, 10
- [ ] ClassZone.com

Steps to Follow

- [ ] Study the vocabulary of **Presentación de vocabulario** (L1 pp. 410–411, L1B pp. 228–230) by reading the captions of the photos. Watch the DVD and complete the video activities copymasters.
- [ ] Use TXT CD 8 tracks 1 and 2 to listen to the vocabulary lesson and the **¡A responder!** activity on page 411 (L1B p. 230; LIB TXT CD 2 track 11).
- [ ] Practice the words of the **Más vocabulario** box on page 411 (L1B p. 230). Read the words aloud. Then write the words in your notebook.
- [ ] Do **Práctica de vocabulario**. Complete **Actividades 1** and **2** on page 412 (L1B p. 231).
- [ ] Complete *Cuaderno* pages 344, 345, and 346 (L1B pp. 148–150).
  OR
  Complete *Cuaderno para hispanohablantes* pages 344, 345, 346, and 347 (L1B pp. 148–151).
- [ ] Check your comprehension by completing the **Para y piensa** box on page 412 (L1B p. 231).
- [ ] Complete Did You Get It? Copymasters 1, 2, and 10.

If You Don't Understand . . .

- [ ] Watch the DVD in a quiet place. Pause and go back if you get lost. Watch it several times.
- [ ] Listen to the CD and imitate the voices and accents of the people on the recording.
- [ ] Use the Interactive Flashcards to help you learn the vocabulary better.

Absent Student Copymasters

Level 1 pp. 413–414
Level 1B pp. 232–233

Vocabulario en contexto

Materials Checklist

- [ ] Student text
- [ ] DVD 2
- [ ] Video activities copymasters
- [ ] TXT CD 8 track 3
- [ ] Did You Get It? Copymasters 1, 3, 11

Steps to Follow

- [ ] Look at the photos on page 413 (L1B p. 232).
- [ ] Read **Cuando escuchas** and **Cuando lees** for **Telehistoria escena 1** on page 413 (L1B p. 232). Copy the questions.
- [ ] Look at the dialogue in the book, then follow along in the book as you listen to TXT CD 8 track 3. Try to understand the dialogue using the pictures and the context.
- [ ] Watch the DVD for **Unidad 8**, **Telehistoria escena 1** without your book. Then watch the DVD again and complete the video activities copymasters.
- [ ] Complete **Actividades 3** and **4** on page 414 (L1B p. 233). Use the CD to help you with **Actividad 3**.
- [ ] Check your comprehension by completing the **Para y piensa** box on page 414 (L1B p. 233).
- [ ] Complete Did You Get It? Copymasters 1, 3, and 11.

If You Don't Understand . . .

- [ ] Watch the DVD and listen to the CD in a quiet place. If you get lost, stop and go back.
- [ ] Read and follow the model before starting so you know what to do.
- [ ] Read aloud everything that you write to make sure that it says what you wanted to say.
- [ ] If you have any questions, write them down so you can ask your teacher later.
- [ ] If you need a partner to complete the activity, practice both parts.

Absent Student Copymasters

Presentación / Práctica de gramática

Materials Checklist

☐ Student text

☐ *Cuaderno* pages 347–349 (L1B pp. 151–153)

☐ *Cuaderno para hispanohablantes* pages 348–350 (L1B pp. 152–154)

☐ Did You Get It? Copymasters 4, 5, 12

☐ ClassZone.com

Steps to Follow

☐ Study the reflexive verbs such as **lavarse** and **acostarse** (L1 p. 415, L1B p. 234).

☐ Do **Actividades 5**, **6**, **7**, and **8** in the text (pp. 416–417, L1B pp. 235–236).

☐ Complete **Actividades 9** and **10** (L1B pp. 236–237).

☐ Complete *Cuaderno* pages 347, 348, and 349 (L1B pp. 151–153).
OR
Complete *Cuaderno para hispanohablantes* pages 348, 349, and 350
(L1B pp. 152–154).

☐ Check your comprehension by completing the **Para y piensa** box on page 417
(L1B p. 237).

☐ Complete Did You Get It? Copymasters 4, 5, and 12.

If You Don't Understand . . .

☐ Reread the activity directions and look at the models several times.

☐ Use the model as a starting point for your own sentences.

☐ Think about what you want to say before writing down your sentences.

☐ Read aloud everything that you write. Be sure that you understand what you
are reading.

☐ Keep a list of questions about anything that is unclear to ask your teacher later.

☐ Practice both parts in partner activities.

☐ Use the Animated Grammar to help you understand.

☐ Use the Leveled Grammar Practice on the @Home Tutor.

Absent Student Copymasters

UNIDAD 8 Lección 1

Absent Student Copymasters

Gramática en contexto

Materials Checklist

☐ Student text

☐ DVD 2

☐ Video activities copymasters

☐ TXT CD 8 tracks 4–6

☐ LIB TXT CD 2 track 12

☐ Did You Get It? Copymasters 4, 6

Steps to Follow

☐ Look at the photo on page 418 (L1B p. 238).

☐ Read **Cuando lees** and **Cuando escuchas** on page 418 (L1B p. 238). Copy the questions.

☐ Read the script and try to understand the dialogue based on the picture.

☐ Listen to **Telehistoria escena 2** on TXT CD 8 track 4 and follow along in your book.

☐ Watch the DVD for **Unidad 8**, **Telehistoria escena 2** without your book. Then watch the DVD again and complete the video activities copymasters.

☐ Study the words in the **También se dice** box.

☐ Complete **Actividades 9** and **10** on page 419. Listen to TXT CD 8 track 5 for **Actividad 10**.

☐ Do **Actividades 11** and **12** (L1B p. 239). Use L1B TXT CD 2 track 12 to complete **Actividad 12**.

☐ Listen to TXT CD 8 track 6 as you follow along in the **Pronunciación** activity on page 419 (L1B p. 239).

☐ Check your comprehension by completing the **Para y piensa** box on page 419 (L1B p. 239).

☐ Complete Did You Get It? Copymasters 4 and 6.

If You Don't Understand . . .

☐ Go to a quiet place and watch the DVD. If you get lost, pause it and go back.

☐ Listen to the CD where you don't have other distractions. Pause and go back as necessary.

☐ Read the directions for each activity several times, and use the models as guides.

Absent Student Copymasters

Presentación / Práctica de gramática

Materials Checklist

☐ Student text

☐ *Cuaderno* pages 350–352 (L1B pp. 154–156)

☐ *Cuaderno para hispanohablantes* pages 351–354 (L1B pp. 155–158)

☐ Did You Get It? Copymasters 7, 8, 10, 11

☐ ClassZone.com

Steps to Follow

☐ Study the present progressive tense for **-ar**, **-er**, and **-ir** verbs.

☐ Do **Actividades 11**, **12**, **13**, and **14** on pages 421 and 422.

☐ Do **Actividades 13**, **14**, **15**, **16**, **17**, and **18** (L1B pp. 241–243).

☐ Complete *Cuaderno* pages 350, 351, and 352 (L1B pp. 154–156).
OR
Complete *Cuaderno para hispanohablantes* pages 351, 352, 353, and 354 (L1B pp. 155–158).

☐ Check your comprehension by completing the **Para y piensa** box on page 422 (L1B p. 243).

☐ Complete Did You Get It? Copymasters 7, 8, 10, and 11.

If You Don't Understand . . .

☐ Reread the activity directions and look at the models several times.

☐ Use the model as a starting point for your own sentences.

☐ Think about what you want to say before writing down your sentences.

☐ Keep a list of questions about anything that is unclear to ask your teacher later.

☐ Practice both parts in partner activities.

☐ Use the Animated Grammar to help you understand.

☐ Use the Leveled Grammar Practice on the @Home Tutor.

Absent Student Copymasters

Todo junto

Materials Checklist

☐ Student text

☐ DVD 2

☐ Video activities copymasters

☐ *Cuaderno* pages 353–354 (L1B pp. 157–158)

☐ *Cuaderno para hispanohablantes* pages 355–356 (L1B pp. 159–160)

☐ TXT CD 8 tracks 7–9

☐ LIB TXT CD 2 tracks 13–14

☐ WB CD 4 tracks 21–24

☐ HL CD 2 tracks 25–28

☐ Did You Get It? Copymasters 7, 9, 10

Steps to Follow

☐ Read **Cuando escuchas** and **Cuando lees** on page 423 (L1B p. 244). Copy the questions.

☐ Review the content of **Unidad 8**, **Telehistoria escena 1** and **escena 2**.

☐ Read the script of **Escena 3** and try to understand the dialogue based on the picture.

☐ Read the script again as you listen to TXT CD 8 track 7.

☐ Watch the DVD for **Unidad 8**, **Telehistoria escena 3** without your book. Then watch the DVD again and complete the video activities copymasters.

☐ Complete **Actividades 15**, **16**, **17**, **18**, and **19** on pages 424 and 425.

☐ Complete **Actividades 19**, **20**, **21**, **22**, and **23** (L1B pp. 244–246).

☐ Complete *Cuaderno* pages 353 and 354 (L1B pp. 157–158).
OR
Complete *Cuaderno para hispanohablantes* pages 355 and 356
(L1B pp. 159–160).

☐ Check your comprehension by completing the **Para y piensa** box on page 425
(L1B p. 246).

☐ Complete Did You Get It? Copymasters 7, 9, and 10.

Absent Student Copymasters

Level 1 pp. 426–428
Level 1B pp. 248–250

Lectura y Conexiones

Materials Checklist

☐ Student text

☐ TXT CD 8 track 10

Steps to Follow

☐ Read **¡Avanza!** Follow the *Strategy*: **Leer** instructions. (L1 p. 426, L1B p. 248)

☐ Read the feature **Mi viaje a Costa Rica**. (L1 pp. 426–427, L1B pp. 248–249)

☐ Follow along with the text on TXT CD 8 track 10.

☐ Check your comprehension by completing the **¿Comprendiste?** and **¿Y tú?** sections of the **Para y piensa** box on page 427 (L1B p. 249).

☐ Read **¡Vamos al museo!** on page 428 (L1B p. 250).

☐ Read **Proyecto 1**, **Las matemáticas**. Do the calculations.

☐ Read **Proyecto 2**, **El lenguaje**, and research the word roots.

☐ Make the poster for **El arte**.

If You Don't Understand . . .

☐ Listen to the CD in a comfortable, quiet place. Pause and go back as often as necessary to keep up with the text.

☐ Read the selection carefully. Use the photos from the album to help you follow the text.

☐ Make a list of questions so you can ask your teacher later.

☐ Review the feature before you write your answer. Think about different ways to state your answer, and choose the best one.

☐ After you write your sentence, look it over to make sure that it says what you wanted to say.

Absent Student Copymasters

UNIDAD 8 Lección 1

Absent Student Copymasters

Repaso de la lección

Materials Checklist

- [ ] Student text
- [ ] *Cuaderno* pages 355–366 (L1B pp. 159–170)
- [ ] *Cuaderno para hispanohablantes* pages 357–366 (L1B pp. 161–170)
- [ ] TXT CD 8 track 11
- [ ] LIB TXT CD 2 track 15
- [ ] WB CD 4 tracks 25–30

Steps to Follow

- [ ] Read the bullet points under **¡Llegada!** on page 430 (L1B p. 252).
- [ ] Complete **Actividades 1**, **2**, **3**, **4**, and **5** (L1 pp. 430–431; L1B pp. 252–253).
- [ ] Complete *Cuaderno* pages 355, 356, and 357. (L1B pp. 159–161).
- [ ] Complete *Cuaderno* pages 358, 359, and 360 (L1B pp. 162–164).
  OR
  Complete *Cuaderno para hispanohablantes* pages 357, 358, 359, and 360
  (L1B pp. 161–164).
- [ ] Complete *Cuaderno* pages 361, 362, and 363 (L1B pp. 165–167).
  OR
  Complete *Cuaderno para hispanohablantes* pages 361, 362, and 363
  (L1B pp. 165–167).
- [ ] Complete *Cuaderno* pages 364, 365, and 366 (L1B pp. 168–170).
  OR
  Complete *Cuaderno para hispanohablantes* pages 364, 365, and 366
  (L1B pp. 168–170).

If You Don't Understand . . .

- [ ] Reread the activity directions several times. Make sure you understand the activity before beginning.
- [ ] For **Actividad 1**, listen to the CD in a quiet place. If you get lost, pause the CD and go back.
- [ ] Read the models silently and aloud to help you understand how to complete each activity.
- [ ] Look up any words you don't understand to find out their meaning.

Copyright © by McDougal Littell, a division of Houghton Mifflin Company.

Absent Student Copymasters

Presentación / Práctica de vocabulario

Materials Checklist

- [ ] Student text
- [ ] DVD 2
- [ ] Video activities copymasters
- [ ] TXT CD 8 tracks 12–13
- [ ] LIB TXT CD 2 track 16
- [ ] *Cuaderno* pages 367–369 (L1B pp. 171–173)
- [ ] *Cuaderno para hispanohablantes* pages 367–370 (L1B pp. 171–174)
- [ ] Did You Get It? Copymasters 13, 14
- [ ] ClassZone.com

Steps to Follow

- [ ] Study the vocabulary of **Presentación de vocabulario** (L1 pp. 434–435; L1B pp. 256–258) by reading the captions of the photos. Watch the DVD and complete the video activities copymasters.

- [ ] Use TXT CD 8 tracks 12 and 13 to listen to the vocabulary lesson (L1 pp. 434–435; L1B pp. 256–258), and do the **¡A responder!** activity (L1 p. 435, L1B p. 258; L1B TXT CD 2 track 16).

- [ ] Practice the words in the **Más vocabulario** box on page 434 (L1B p. 256). Read the words aloud. Write the words in your notebook.

- [ ] In **Práctica de vocabulario**, complete **Actividades 1** and **2** on page 436 (L1B p. 259).

- [ ] Complete *Cuaderno* pages 367, 368, and 369 (L1B pp. 171–173).
  OR
  Complete *Cuaderno para hispanohablantes* pages 367, 368, 369, and 370 (L1B pp. 171–174).

- [ ] Check your comprehension by completing the **Para y piensa** box on page 436 (L1B p. 259).

- [ ] Complete Did You Get It? Copymasters 13 and 14.

If You Don't Understand . . .

- [ ] Watch the DVD in a quiet place. Play it again if you get lost. Watch it several times.

- [ ] Listen to the CD and imitate the voices and accents of the people on the recording.

- [ ] Use the Interactive Flashcards to reinforce the vocabulary.

UNIDAD 8 Lección 2

Absent Student Copymasters

Absent Student Copymasters

Level 1 pp. 437–438
Level 1B pp. 260–261

Vocabulario en contexto

Materials Checklist

☐ Student text

☐ DVD 2

☐ Video activities copymasters

☐ TXT CD 8 track 14

☐ Did You Get It? Copymasters 13, 15

Steps to Follow

☐ Look at the photos on page 437.

☐ Read **Cuando lees** and **Cuando escuchas** for **Telehistoria escena 1** on page 437 (L1B p. 260). Copy the questions.

☐ Look at the dialogue in the book, then follow along in the book as you listen to TXT CD 8 track 14. Try to understand the dialogue using the pictures and the context.

☐ Watch the DVD for **Unidad 8**, **Telehistoria escena 2** without your book. Then watch the DVD again and complete the video activities copymasters.

☐ Complete **Actividades 3** and **4** on page 438 (L1B p. 261). Use the CD to help you with **Actividad 3**.

☐ Check your comprehension by completing the **Para y piensa** box on page 438 (L1B p. 261).

☐ Complete Did You Get It? Copymasters 13 and 15.

If You Don't Understand . . .

☐ Watch the DVD and listen to the CD in a quiet place. If you get lost, stop and go back.

☐ Use the models to help you understand how to make your own sentences and answers.

☐ Read aloud everything that you write to make sure that it says what you wanted to say.

☐ If you have any questions, write them down so you can ask your teacher later.

☐ In **Actividad 4**, write and practice the parts of both partners.

Absent Student Copymasters

Presentación / Práctica de gramática

Materials Checklist

☐ Student text

☐ *Cuaderno* pages 370–372 (L1B pp. 174–176)

☐ *Cuaderno para hispanohablantes* pages 371–373 (L1B pp. 175–177)

☐ Did You Get It? Copymasters 16, 17, 22, 23

☐ ClassZone.com

Steps to Follow

☐ Study the indirect object pronouns on page 439 (L1B p. 262). Say them aloud several times.

☐ Do **Actividades 5**, **6**, **7**, and **8** in the text (L1 pp. 440–441; L1B pp. 263–264).

☐ Complete **Actividades 9**, **10**, and **11** (L1B p. 265).

☐ Complete *Cuaderno* pages 370, 371, and 372 (L1B pp. 174–176).
OR
Complete *Cuaderno para hispanohablantes* pages 371, 372, and 373 (L1B pp. 175–177).

☐ Check your comprehension by completing the **Para y piensa** box on page 441 (L1B p. 265).

☐ Complete Did You Get It? Copymasters 16, 17, 22, and 23.

If You Don't Understand . . .

☐ Reread the activity directions and look at the models several times.

☐ Use the model as a starting point for your own sentences. Study the sentence structure before you write your sentences.

☐ Think about what you want to say before writing your sentences.

☐ Read the text and your answers two or three times. Check for spelling and punctuation marks.

☐ Keep a list of questions about anything that is unclear to ask your teacher later.

☐ Use the Animated Grammar to help you understand.

☐ Use the Leveled Grammar Practice on the @Home Tutor.

Absent Student Copymasters

Level 1 pp. 442–443
Level 1B pp. 266–267

Gramática en contexto

Materials Checklist

- [ ] Student text
- [ ] DVD 2
- [ ] Video activities copymasters
- [ ] TXT CD 8 tracks 15–16
- [ ] Did You Get It? Copymasters 16, 18, 23

Steps to Follow

- [ ] Look at the photo on page 442 (L1B p. 266).
- [ ] Read **Cuando lees** and **Cuando escuchas** on page 442 (L1B p. 266). Copy the questions.
- [ ] Read the script and try to understand the dialogue based on the picture.
- [ ] Listen to **Telehistoria escena 2** on TXT CD 8 track 15 and follow along in your book.
- [ ] Watch the DVD for **Unidad 8**, **Telehistoria escena 2** without your book. Then watch the DVD again and complete the video activities copymasters.
- [ ] Study the words in the **También se dice** box.
- [ ] Complete **Actividades 9** and **10** on page 443. Do the parts of both partners in **Actividad 10**.
- [ ] Complete **Actividades 12** and **13** (L1B p. 267). Practice the role of both partners in **Actividad 13**.
- [ ] Listen to TXT CD 8 track 16 as you follow along in the **Pronunciación** activity on page 443 (L1B p. 267).
- [ ] Check your comprehension by completing the **Para y piensa** box on page 443 (L1B p. 267).
- [ ] Complete Did You Get It? Copymasters 16, 18, and 23.

If You Don't Understand . . .

- [ ] Go to a quiet place and watch the DVD. If you get lost, stop and play it again.
- [ ] Listen to the CD where you don't have other distractions. Pause and go back as necessary.
- [ ] Read the directions for each activity several times, and use the models as guides.
- [ ] Read aloud everything that you write. Be sure that you understand what you are reading.

Absent Student Copymasters

Presentación / Práctica de gramática

Materials Checklist

☐ Student text

☐ *Cuaderno* pages 373–375 (L1B pp. 177–179)

☐ *Cuaderno para hispanohablantes* pages 374–377 (L1B pp. 178–181)

☐ TXT CD 8 track 17

☐ LIB TXT CD 2 track 17

☐ Did You Get It? Copymasters 19, 20, 22, 24

☐ ClassZone.com

Steps to Follow

☐ Study the demonstrative adjectives on page 444 (L1B p. 268).

☐ Do **Actividades 11**, **12**, **13**, and **14** on pages 445 and 446, using TXT CD 8 track 17 for **Actividad 12**.

☐ Complete **Actividades 14**, **15**, **16**, **17**, **18**, and **19** (L1B pp. 269–271). Use LIB TXT CD 2 track 17 to do **Actividad 15**.

☐ Complete *Cuaderno* pages 373, 374, and 375 (L1B pp. 177–179).
OR
Complete *Cuaderno para hispanohablantes* pages 374, 375, 376, and 377 (L1B pp. 178–181).

☐ Check your comprehension by completing the **Para y piensa** box on page 446 (L1B p. 271).

☐ Complete Did You Get It? Copymasters 19, 20, 22, and 24.

If You Don't Understand . . .

☐ Reread the activity directions and look at the models several times.

☐ Use the model as a starting point for your own sentences. Study the sentence structure before you write your sentences.

☐ Practice both parts of the partner activities (such as **Actividad 14**).

☐ Use the Animated Grammar to help you understand.

☐ Use the Leveled Grammar Practice on the @Home Tutor.

Absent Student Copymasters

Todo junto

Materials Checklist

- [ ] Student text
- [ ] DVD 2
- [ ] Video activities copymasters
- [ ] *Cuaderno* pages 376–377 (L1B pp. 180–181)
- [ ] *Cuaderno para hispanohablantes* pages 378–379 (L1B pp. 182–183)
- [ ] TXT CD 8 tracks 18–20
- [ ] LIB TXT CD 2 tracks 18–19
- [ ] WB CD 4 tracks 31–34
- [ ] HL CD 2 tracks 29–32
- [ ] Did You Get It? Copymasters 19, 21

Steps to Follow

- [ ] Read **Cuando escuchas** and **Cuando lees** on page 447 (L1B p. 272). Copy the questions.

- [ ] Review the content of **Unidad 8**, **Telehistoria escena 1** and **escena 2**.

- [ ] Read the script of **Escena 3** and try to understand the dialogue based on the picture.

- [ ] Read the script again as you listen to TXT CD 8 track 18.

- [ ] Watch the DVD for **Unidad 8**, **Telehistoria escena 3** without your book. Then watch the DVD again and complete the video activities copymasters.

- [ ] Complete **Actividades 15**, **16**, **17**, **18**, and **19** (pp. 448–449). Practice the parts of both partners in **Actividad 17**.

- [ ] Complete **Actividades 20**, **21**, **22**, **23**, and **24** (L1B pp. 273–274).

- [ ] Complete *Cuaderno* pages 376 and 377 (L1B pp. 180–181).
  OR
  Complete *Cuaderno para hispanohablantes* pages 378 and 379
  (L1B pp. 182–183).

- [ ] Check your comprehension by completing the **Para y piensa** box on page 449 (L1B p. 274).

- [ ] Complete Did You Get It? Copymasters 19 and 21.

Absent Student Copymasters

Lectura cultural

Materials Checklist

☐ Student text

☐ TXT CD 8 track 21

Steps to Follow

☐ Read the *Strategy*: **Leer** (L1 p. 450, L1B p. 276).

☐ Read **Mercados en Costa Rica y Uruguay** on pages 450 and 451 (L1B pp. 276–277).

☐ Follow along with the text on TXT CD 8 track 21.

☐ Check your comprehension by completing the **¿Comprendiste?** and **¿Y tú?** sections of the **Para y piensa** box on page 451 (L1B p. 277).

If You Don't Understand . . .

☐ Rewind and pause the CD as often as necessary. Listen in a quiet place.

☐ Read the questions several times. Read them aloud as well as silently.

☐ Think about several ways to answer the questions. Choose the one that best says what you want to say.

☐ Make a list of questions if any words or sentences are unclear.

Absent Student Copymasters

Level 1 p. 452
Level 1B p. 278

Proyectos culturales

Materials Checklist

☐ Student text

Steps to Follow

☐ Read **Postres en Costa Rica y Uruguay** and look at the illustrations.
(L1 p. 452, L1B 278)

☐ Read the description and recipe for **Plátanos horneados** in **Proyecto 1**. Make them, if you can, with adult supervision.

☐ Read the description and recipe for **Dulce de leche** in **Proyecto 2**. Make it, if possible and if you have permission.

If You Don't Understand . . .

☐ Read the activity directions a few times, both silently and aloud.

☐ If you have any doubts or observations, write them down so you can discuss them with your teacher later.

☐ Prepare all your ingredients ahead of time. Have an adult help you with any activities that involve the oven.

Absent Student Copymasters

Repaso de la lección

Materials Checklist

☐ Student text

☐ *Cuaderno* pages 378–389 (L1B pp. 182–193)

☐ *Cuaderno para hispanohablantes* pages 380–389 (L1B pp. 184–193)

☐ TXT CD 8 track 22

☐ LIB TXT CD 2 track 20

☐ WB CD 4 tracks 35–40

Steps to Follow

☐ Read the bullet points under **¡Llegada!** on page 454 (L1B p. 280).

☐ Complete **Actividades 1**, **2**, **3**, **4**, and **5** (L1 pp. 454–455, L1B pp. 280–281).

☐ Complete *Cuaderno* pages 378, 379, and 380 (L1B pp. 182–184).

☐ Complete *Cuaderno* pages 381, 382, and 383 (L1B pp. 185–187).
OR
Complete *Cuaderno para hispanohablantes* pages 380, 381, 382, and 383 (L1B pp. 184–187).

☐ Complete *Cuaderno* pages 384, 385, and 386 (L1B pp. 188–190).
OR
Complete *Cuaderno para hispanohablantes* pages 384, 385, and 386 (L1B pp. 188–190).

☐ Complete *Cuaderno* pages 387, 388, and 389 (L1B pp. 191–193).
OR
Complete *Cuaderno para hispanohablantes* pages 387, 388, and 389 (L1B pp. 191–193).

If You Don't Understand . . .

☐ Reread the activity directions several times. Review the model. Put the directions in your own words.

☐ For **Actividad 1**, listen to the CD in a quiet place. If you get lost, pause the CD and go back.

☐ Read the models silently and aloud to help you understand how to complete each activity.

☐ Look up any words you don't understand to find out their meaning.

Absent Student Copymasters

Comparación cultural

Materials Checklist

☐ Student text

☐ TXT CD 8 track 23

Steps to Follow

☐ Read the directions in **Lectura y escritura** for **Actividades 1** and **2** on page 456 (L1B p. 282).

☐ Listen to TXT CD 8 track 23 as you read **¡De vacaciones!** in the text (L1 p. 457, L1B p. 283).

☐ Read the strategy for **Escribir**, then begin **Actividad 2**.

☐ Complete the **Compara con tu mundo** section on page 456 (L1B p. 282).

If You Don't Understand . . .

☐ Look over all the instructions for **Leer** and **Escribir** before you begin to read the feature.

☐ Listen to the CD in a quiet place. Pause and go back as often as necessary. Repeat unfamiliar words aloud.

☐ Look up words you don't know. Keep a list of new vocabulary.

☐ If you get confused, make a list of questions to ask your teacher later.

☐ Think about what you want to say before you begin writing. Reread everything you write. Check for punctuation, spelling, and verb–subject agreement.

Absent Student Copymasters

Repaso inclusivo

Materials Checklist

☐ Student text

☐ TXT CD 8 track 24

Steps to Follow

☐ Use TXT CD 8 track 24 to complete **Actividad 1** on page 458 (L1B p. 284). Imitate the voices on the CD.

☐ Complete **Actividades 2**, **3**, **4**, **5**, **6**, and **7** (L1 pp. 458–459, L1B pp. 284–285).

If You Don't Understand . . .

☐ For **Actividad 1**, listen to the CD in a quiet place. If you get lost, pause the CD and go back.

☐ Use the textbook and review the vocabulary and verb conjugations you need to complete each activity.

☐ Write and practice the parts of both partners in all activities that call for partner work.

☐ Think about what you want to say before you begin to write. Make sure that it makes sense. Read aloud everything that you write.

☐ If you have any questions, write them down for your teacher to answer later.